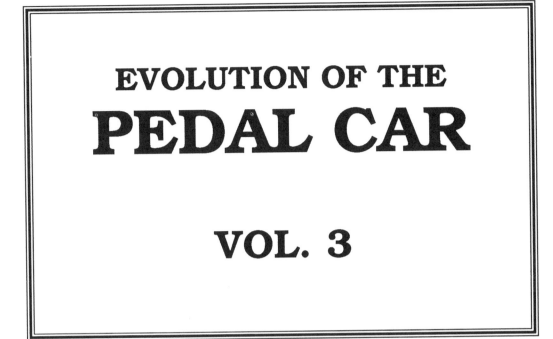

EVOLUTION OF THE
PEDAL CAR

VOL. 3

Edited by Neil S. Wood

© Copyright 1992

📖 **L-W BOOK SALES** 📖

P.O. Box 69
Gas City, IN 46933

ISBN# 0-89538-006-4

TABLE OF CONTENTS

The Car On The Front Cover Is a 1941 Steelcraft Chrysler

Introduction

Children's Pedal Car interest has grown in the past few years to an almost unbelievable proportion. It is one of the most desirable, fastest appreciating collectibles to be found today. It is now an adult toy.

There were five well known early manufacturers of pedal cars; American National, Gendron, Steelcraft, Garton and Toledo Wheel. These companies are all out of business today. Deluxe pedal cars were only bought by the wealthy in the 1920s and 1930s making it very difficult to find one in really good condition. Some full size car collectors are selling their collections and going into pedal car collecting since there is no maintenance to pedal cars.

Pedal cars of the 1920s and 1930s are a big part of American history. They have moved from the sidewalks into the living rooms for decorating, displays, etc. They are nice to admire under the Christmas tree for decoration instead of gifts for children. Good luck in your pedaling !

→ Pricing ←

The price guide in this book is for Pedal Cars in good to excellent condition. Cars found with parts missing, very poor paint, wheels changed from originals, or excessive rust will bring much lower prices. A car considered to be in good condition is one with original paint and no parts missing. A car in excellent condition is one that is 70% to 95% mint. This price guide is based on cars in these conditions. L-W books can not be responsible for gains or losses, as this is ONLY A GUIDE.

We would like to thank everyone who sent us pictures and information. If we could not use your picture because of quality or other reason we are truly sorry. We also had some problems reading some addresses and names and hope that we came up with the correct information. If we did make a mistake on your pedal car information please accept our apology.

Thank You

Darwin Hunkler, David Dilley (our layout man),Paul & Naomi Premer for the exceptional front cover and a special thanks to Elmer Duellman and Randall Arterburn. I bothered Elmer and Randall both night and day and would have been lost without their advice.

So to all

Thanks

COLLECTORS & CONTRIBUTORS

Accarpio,Paul & Linda - 369 Hackmatack Street - Manchester,Conn. 06040
Albert,Ray - 170A Spahr-Seiling Rd.#2 - Dillsburg,PA 17019
Applegate,Dean - 6531 Downs Rd. - Warren,OH 44481
Arrington,Harold & Judy - Box 46 - Levelland,TX 79336
Arrington,Harold & Judy - Box 1547 - Wichita Falls,TX 76307
Arterburn,Randy - 21 South Addison - Indianapolis,IN 46222
Aust,Ronald - 3715 Volquardsen Ave. - Davenport,IA 52806
Barry,David - P.O.Box 46 - Epping,NSW 2121,Australia
Bennett,Kevin - P.O.Box 1523 - Zillah,WA 98953
Bio,Richard - 63 Health Ave. - Providence,RI 02908
Blanchard,John - 171 Great Rd. - Littleton,Mass 01460
Block,Todd - 603 Inverness - St.Peter,MN 56082
Breeze,Rodney - 302 Ft.Sill Blvd. - Lawton,OK 73501
Brown,David & Erica - 51 King St. - St.Augustine,FL 32084
Brown,Roberta - 815 W.Cypress - Redlands,CA 92373
Buchanan,John - 671 S. Water - Marine City,MI 48039
Burt,Gene - Rd.1,Box 302 - Pleasantville,PA 16341
Buske,Earl R. - P.O.Box 129 - Pocohontas,IA 50574
Cain,E.G. - 8603 Butler-Warren - West Chester,OH 45069
Castelli,Steve - P.O.Box 559 - Windsor,CA 95492
Chaussee,Calvin - 1530 Kenland Ct. - Colorado Springs,CO 80915
Cirkl,Larry - 100 West Main St. - Robins,Iowa 52328
Clemens,Rick - 24481 S. Larkin Rd. - Beavercreek,OR 97004
Colligan,Bob & Pamela - 10 Fernwood Dr. - Loudonville,NY 12211
Cristando,John - 836 Connie La. - Elmont,NY 11003
Dalmatoff,Alex - 5429 N. San Marcos - Fresno,CA 93722
Davis,Richard - 709 W. Kingsley - Garland,TX 75041
Davis,Thomas - 322 E Vista - Garlnd,TX 75041
Davis,Timothy Joe - 8731 Stanwood - Dallas,TX 75228
Depenbrok,Bob - 9665 Venna Ave. - Arleta,CA 91331
Dickson,Dennis - 2788 10th Street - Lebanon,OR 97355
Dodd,Richard - 629 S. Scenic - Springfield,MO 65802
Domanik,Joe - 6501 River Meadows Turn - Racine,WI 53402
Donahue,Greg & Karyl - 12900 S.Betty Point - Floral City,FL 32636
Doster,Veronica A. - P.O.Box 287 - Athens,GA 30603
Duellman,Elmer - Rt.2,Box 26 - Fountain City,WI 54629
Ebersole,O.S. - Box 56,Rd. 3 - Hummelstown,PA 17036
Ellsworth,Bob - 1207 Charter Oak Dr. - Taylors,SC 29687
Elwell,Mike - 7412 Iden Ave. So. - Cottage Grove,MN 55016
Endres,Terry - P.O.Box 22 - Ft.Collins,CO 80522
Erckens,Fritz - D-51 Aachen - Krämerstrabe 23 - Deutschland
Farnham,Larry & Betty - 6650 Jackson St. N.E. - Minneapolis,MN 55432
Fisher,Danny - 1921 Castle Dr. - Garland,TX 75040
Fitzgerald,Dan & Jan - 11021 Hudson Ct. - Thornton,CO 80233
Fork,Harriet - 1403 NCR 32 - Gibsonburg,OH 43431
Forster,Fred & Rosanne - 22 Pine Cliff Lake Dr. - West Milford,NJ 07480
Funkhouser,Ron - Rt.1,Box 496 - Tomsbrook,VA 22660
Geary,Jim - Rt.14,Box 125 - Goldsboro,NC 27530
Giolma,Clive - 700 Downie St. - Kamloops,BC,Can. V2B 5T2
Glerum,Jay - 1483 Casa Park Circle - Winter Springs,FL 32708
Gordon,Frank & Irlene - 9622 Lee Blvd. - Leawood,KA 66206
Gottenborg,Phil - 839 E. Fremont - Galesburg,IL 61401
Guggemos,Bill - 1104 N. Creyts Rd. - Lansing,MI 48917

Guiney,Patrick - 46 Cathedral Circle - Nashua,NH 03063
Hagevran,Marc - Zilvrmos 27 - 2914 XK Nieuwerkerk a/d IJssel - The Netherlands
Harvieux,Jerry - 13716 Wellington Crescent - Burnsville,MN 55337
Hauschka,Kurt - 116 Chaberlain St. - Rochester,NH 03867
Haver,George & Laurie - 8585 Sheridan Dr. - Williamsville,NY 14221
Holder,Kerry - 4064 Northwood Dr. - Springfield,MO 65003
Hooley,Frank - 1908 Burdell - Troy,NY 12180
Huffhines,David - 701 Gatewood Dr. - Garland,TX 75043
Hughes,Blake - 6848 Donahoo - Kansas City,KS 66104
Hunkler,Darwin - R.R.2,Box 198 - Russiaville,IN 46901
Jestes,Ken & Jill - 11311 Lake Tree Court - Boca Raton,FL 33498
Johnson,Wanda - 465 Simon Ave - Kingman,AZ 86401
Juenemann,Roy - 6024 Sullivan - Wichita,KS 67204
Karpinen,Daniel - 95-06 99th Ave. - Queens,NY 11417
Katason,Greg - 3857 Shoshore - Denver,CO 80211
Keehn,Charles - 540 Kinderkamack Rd. - River Edge,NJ 07661
Kellar,Bob - 61 Macon St. - Sayville,NY 11782
Kent,Danny - P.O.Box 1046 - Eaton Park,FL 33840
King,Dick - 1811 Baker Way Loop - Kelso,WA 98626
Kirk,Joe - 551 Central Ave. - Shafter,CA 93263
Kirsch,Gene - 2074 Western Ave. No. - Roseville,MN 55113
Klang,Don & Betty - 1102 E. 59th St. - Tacoma,WA 98404
Knox,Don - 1941 Vinland Rd. - Oshkosh,WI 54901
Koch,Michael - 495 Dallas Dr. - Thousand Oaks,CA 91360
Kyber,Robert - 14 Lake Rd. - Chatham Township,NJ 07928
Laduca,David - 5138 Daha Dr. - Lewiston,NY 14092
Lambrecht,Robert - 2625 Clark Ave. - Billings,Mont. 59102
Lampman,Bob & Betty - P.O.Box 566 - Veron,NY 13476
Leopard,David M. - 2507 Feather Run Trail - West Columbia,SC 29169-4915
Lineback,M.K. - 1905 Potomac Dr. - Greensboro,NC 27403
Linkous,Blaine - P.O..Box 178 - Fallston,MD 21047
Lynch,Bill - 2330 Elm - Bellingham,WA 98225
McKenzie,John - P.O.Box 111 - Seal Beach,CA 90740
Meadors,Gary - P.O.Box 424 - Alamo,CA 94507
Memory Lane Classics - 12551 Jefferson St. - Perrysburg,OH 43551
Mitchell,Wayne A. - P.O.Box 100 - Keller,TX 76248
Morrow,Daniel - Rt. Box 70 - Fleming,OH 45729
Mowrey,Jan - 831 South 51st St. - Lincoln,NE 68510
Neal,Harold - Rt.2,Box 76 - McDonald,TN 37353
Olivers Auction Gallery - Rt.1,Plaza One - Kennebunk,ME 04043
Paone,Michael - P.O.Box 18 - Berkeley Hgts.,NJ 07922
Parker,Chas - Rd.2,Box368 - Tarentum,PA 15084
Parkhurst,Jim - 256 South Ave. - Bridgeton,NJ 08302
Pate,Richard H. - 493 Elm St. - Biddeford,ME 04005
Phillips,Stan - 438 Eighth Street - Oakmont,PA 15139
Pickering,Ron - 1236 So. Ocean Dr. - Ft.Lauderdale,FL 33316
Portell,Dan - Box 91 - Hematite,MO 63047
Powers,Steve - 119 Arden Dr. - So. San Francisco,CA 94080
Premer,Paul & Naomi - P.O.Box 103 - Evans,CO 80620
Rastall,John - P.O.Box 435 - Fraser,MI 48026
Reed,David - P.O.Box 653 - Redding,CT 06896
Reinhardt,John - 885 St.Jean - Florissant,MO 63031
Richter,Dave - 6817 Sutherland - Mentor,OH 44060
Ricker's Antiques - Rd.1 - Mill Hall,PA 17751
Robidoux,Kurt - 1234 S. 9th St. - Lincoln,NE 68502

Rocha,Daniel R. & Kathy - 12318 Turner Circle - Omaha,NE 68123
Roy,Aaron - 817 Edgehill - Ashland,OH 44805
Sandhill Antiques - 1000 W. Main St. - Robins,IA 52328
Sawyer,Dwight - Chatham Auto Body - Chatham,NY
Schaut,Jerome - 216 Grandview - St.Marys,PA 15857
Schneider,Larry - 9476 S. 27th St. - Oak Dreek,WI 53154
Severeid,William - 815 Meridian St. - Mishawaka,IN 46544
Sims,Roseana - 424 Dollins - Cedar hills,TX 75104
Smith,Jim - P.O.Box 472113 - Garland,TX 75047-2113
Smith,Maynard - Rt.2,Box 75 - Scranton,KS 66537
Spadone,Dennis F. - 10 Rose Ct. - Denville,NJ 07834
Stack,Art - 2990 Transit Rd. - Buffalo,NY 14224
Stanley,Lonnie & Connie - 5673 N. Main - Vidor,TX 77662
Steele,Ross - Rt.5,Box 005588 - Madisonville,TN 37354
Stegeman,John - 1434 34th St. - Allegan,MI 49010
Sterling,Kimball - 125 Main St. - Jonesboro,TN 37659
Stoller,Nate & Charlene - 960 Reynolds Ave. - Ripon,CA 95366
Swaney,Bill - Box 152 - Mars,PA 16046
Swink,William - Rt.6,Box 603-B - Morganton,NC 28655
Torel,M.J. - 1620 Palmcroft Dr. SW - Phoenix,AZ 85007
Torres,Peter - 16010 Jensen St. - Granada Hill,CA 91344
Torres,Peter - 16010 Jensen St. - Granada Hill,CA 91344
Traugh,Dick - 299 Norwood Ln. - Grants Pass,OR 97527
Turk,Jerry - 4240 Carvel Ln. - Edgewater,MD 21037
Vesely,Melvin J. - 1645 N. LaGrange Rd. - LaGrange Pk.,IL 60525
Vidaurri,Darrell - 17547 Fernwood Dr. - Jamestown,CA 95327
Vitunic,Tom - 4684 Roland Rd. - Allison Park,PA 15101
Vondrasek,Merle J. - 409 N. Hampton - Desoto,Texas 75115
Vos,Robert - 12139 N.W. 29th St. - Coral Springs,FL 33065
Wattawa,Don - 3578 W. Parnell Ave. - Milwaukee,WI 53221
Wickfelder,Jim - 16934 Cicero - Tinley Park,IL 60477
Wiggins,William - 1926 N. Anderson St. - Tacoma,WA 98406
Wilson,Allen C. - 1709 Santa Cecilia - Kingsville,TX 78363
Zalvd,Herman - P.O.Box 849 - North Platte,NE 69101

CONTRIBUTING DEALERS AND RESTORERS

Applegate,Dean - 6531 Downs Rd. - Warren,OH 44481
Arterburn,Randy - 21 South Addison - Indianapolis,IN 46222
Branch,Charles - Rt.8,Box 524 - Marshall,TX 75670
Brown,Roberta - 815 W.Cypress - Redlands,CA 92373
Bygone Toys by Gordon - 9622 Lee Blvd. - Leawood,KS 66206
Classic Restorations - 1709 Santa Cecilia - Kingsville,TX 78363
Davis,Timothy Joe - 8731 Stanwood - Dallas,TX 75228
Depenbrok,Bob - 9665 Vena Ave. - Arleta,CA 91331
Dodd,Richard - 629 S. Scenic - Springfield,MO 65802
Donahue,Greg - 12900 South Betty Point - Floral City,FL 32636
Duellman,Elmer - Rt.2,Box 26 - Fountain City,WI 54629
Duffy's Collectible Cars - 250 Classic Car Court SW - Cedar Rapids,Iowa 52404
Ellsworth,Bob - 1207 Charter Oak Dr. - Taylors,SC 29687
Elwell,Mike - 7412 Iden Ave So. - Cottage Grove,MN 55016
Farnham,Larry & Betty - 6650 Jackson St. N.E. - Minneapolis,MN 55432
Geary,Jim - Rt.14,Box 125 - Goldsboro,NC 27530

Golden Oak Antiques - 10 Fernwood Dr. - Loudonville,NY 12211
Goodguys - P.O.Box 424 - Alamo,CA 94507
Gottenborg,Phil - 839 E. Fremont - Galesburg,IL 61401
Hemmelman,Harold - R.R.1 - Centerville,Wi 54630
Hidden Treasure Antiques - 327 S. Main St. - Franklin,OH
Hogies Cycle Shop - 1160 Goffle Rd. - Hawthorne,NJ
Holder,Kerry - 4064 Northwood Dr. - Springfield,MO 65003
Hunkler,Darwin - R.R.2,Box 198 - Russiaville,IN 46901
Hurd,james L. - 217 No. Jefferson St. - Chicago,IL 60606
Just Antiques & Collectibles - 3100 Jewell Dr. - Arlington,TX 76016
K.David's Gallery - 51 King St. - St.Augustine,FL 32084
Kasper Auto Trim - 2949 North Lake Dr. - WaterFord,WI 53185
Kent,Danny - P.O.Box 1046 - Eaton Park,FL 33840
King Kraft - 1811 Baker Way Loop - Kelso,WA 98626
Knox,Don - 1941 Vinland Rd. - Oshkosh,WI 54901
L&B Antiques - P.O.Box 158 - Cedarville,OH 45314
Laduca,David - 5138 Daha Dr. - lewiston,NY 14092
Lampman,Robert - Rd#1,Box 73 0 - Vernon,NY 13476
Leopard,David M. - 2507 Feather Run Trail - West Columbia,SC 29169-4915
Lineback & Sons - 1905 Potomac Dr. - Greensboro,NC 27403
Linkous,Blaine - P.O.Box 178 - Fallston,MD 21047
Marschman,Gene - 13243 S.E. Terra Cascade Dr. - Clackamas,OR 97015
Memory Lane Classics - 12551 Jefferson St. - Perrysburg,OH 43551
Mid City Auto & Antiques - 409 N. Hampton - Desoto,Texas 75115
Morrow Collision Inc. - 3681 Elizabeth Lake Rd. - Pontiac,MI 48054
Neals - Rt.2,Box 76 - White Oak Valley Rd. - McDonald,TN 37353
Nestle,Paul - P.O.Box 59 - Nipomo,CA 93444
Olimpio,Marc - P.O..Box 1505 - Wolfeboro,NH 03894
Olivers Auction Gallery - Rt.1,Plaza One - Kennebunk,ME 04043
Paone,Michael - P.O.Box 18 - Berkeley Hgts.,NJ 07922
Pate Motor Co. - U.S. #1 - 493 Elm St. - Biddeford,ME 04005
Pedal Power Toy Co. - 1122 W. Almond Ave. - Orange,CA 92668
Portell Restorations - Box 91 - Hematite,MO 63047
Premer Motors - P.O.Box 103 - Evans,CO 80620
Racioppo & Scala Pedal Vehicles - 314 E. Leasure Ave. - New Castle,PA 16101
Rastall,John - P.O.Box 435 - Fraser,MI 48026
Restoration Plus Inc. - 1808 Pickwick Ln. - Glenview,IL - 60025
Robert Vos & Associates - 12139 N.W. 29th St. - Coral Springs,FL 33065
Sandhill Antiques - 100 West Main St. - Robins,Iowa 52328
Sawyer,Dwight - Chatham Auto Body - Chatham,NY
Schneider,Larry - 9476 S. 27th St. - Oak Creek,WI
Smith,Jim - P.O.Box 472113 - Garland,TX 75047-2113
Stegeman,John - 1434 34th St. - Allegan,MI 49010
Swaney,Bill - Box 152 - Mars,PA 16046
The Harvieux Family - 13716 Wellington Cres. - Burnsville,MN 55337
The Joys of Toys - 815 Meridian St. - Mishawaka,IN 46544
The Rocha Bros. - 154 McRoberts Way - Mather AFB,CA 95655
The Rocha Bros. - 12318 Turner Circle - Omaha,NE 68123
Tony's Collectible Toys - 1007 Pamela Circle - Mainville,OH 45039
Torr,William - 527 White Ave. - Northvale,NJ 07647
Vitunic,Tom - 4684 Roland Rd. - Allison Park,PA 15101
Weirick,Ed - RFD #3,Box 190 - Ellsworth,ME 04605
White,W.Bruce - 70564 Sunrise Dr. - Edwardsburg,MI 49112
Wiggins,William - 1926 N.Anderson St. - Tacoma,WA 98406
Wilson,Allen C. - 1709 Santa Cecilia - Kingsville,TX 78363

Places To Go - Reading To Do

Following are shows you don't want to miss if you are interested in Bicycles, Pedal Cars and related items.

Antique Toy & Doll World, St. Charles, IL, April, June, October
Info: Antique World Shows, Inc., P.O. Box 34509, Chicago, IL 60634
Phone 312-725-0633

INDY ANTIQUE ADVERTISING SHOW, Indiana St. Frgrnds, Indianapolis
March, June, September
Info: Mary Kokles, 6018 Northaven, Dallas, TX 75230
Phone 214-240-1987

Brimfield, Mass. Shows in May, July, and September
Phone 413-245-3436

Greenville, SC Pedal Car & Toy Show, Memorial Weekend
Phone 803-244-4308

Hershey, Pennsylvania, National AACA Meet, October

Kalamazoo, MI, Antique Toy Circus Maximus
3rd Saturday in May, Saturday after Thanksgiving
Info: 1720 Rupert, Grand Rapids, MI 49505
Phone 616-361-9887

Dayton, Ohio M.C.T.A. Show, April & October
Info: M.C.T.A., P.O.Box 403 N.D. Station, Dayton, OH 45404
Phone 513-233-8381

If you deal in Pedal Cars or related items, the following publications will be of interest to you.

Collectors Showcase, P. O. Box 837, Tulsa, OK 74101
Wheel Goods Trader, P. O. Box 435, Fraser, MI 48026
Antique Trader, P. O. Box 1050, Dubuque, IA 52001
Antique Toy World, P. O. Box 34509, Chicago, IL 60634
U. S. Toy Collector, P. O. Box 4244, Missoula, MT 59806
The Inside Collector, 657 Meacham Ave., Elmont, Long Island, N.Y. 11003

ELMER DUELLMAN IS AN ADVANCED COL-
LECTOR. AS USUAL HE IS ALWAYS INTER-
ESTED IN BUYING,SELLING AND TRADING
TO UPGRADE HIS FINE COLLECTION. YOU
MAY CONTACT HIM AT:

ELMER DUELLMAN
RT.2, BOX 26
FOUNTAIN CITY,WI 54629
(608) 687-7221

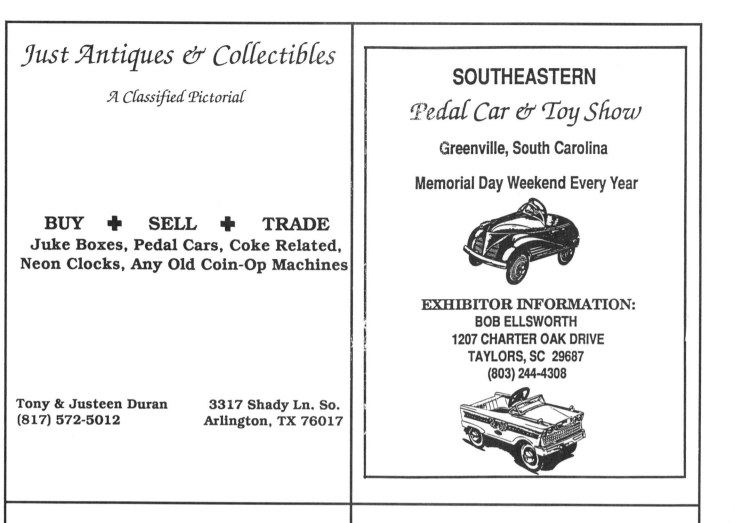

13

14

THE IRISH MAIL LINE

Above is our
REGISTERED TRADE MARK
Look for it on the seat

The way to distinguish the IRISH MAIL from imitations is by our Registered Trade Mark which is the name

"THE IRISH MAIL"

THE above illustrations show an exact reproduction of our registered trade mark "The Irish Mail" and any hand car that does not have this name on the seat is not a genuine Irish Mail.

Any dealer or jobber who advertises or catalogs a hand car that is not the genuine Irish Mail under the name "Irish Mail," or any dealer who sells or offers for sale another make of hand car as the Irish Mail, infringes our registered trade mark and is liable for damages. We urge our dealers to promptly report to us any such infringement that may come to their notice. If a competitor advertises Irish Mail at greatly reduced prices, investigate to see if he is selling the genuine Irish Mail. Usually it is a cheap substitute and we should know about it at once in order to protect our mutual interests.

HILL~STANDARD MFG. CO. · ANDERSON, IND. · U·S·A·

THE IRISH MAIL LINE

JUNIOR IRISH MAIL (Patented)
For Boys and Girls

No.	Price Each	Wheels	Tires	Packed	Weight Per Crate
6		8 and 10-in.	½-in. Rubber	One in Crate	25 lbs.

A Hand Car is not an Irish Mail unless the name "Irish Mail" is on the seat.

A smaller size "IRISH MAIL" suitable for children two to five years of age.

IRISH MAIL DELIVERY

No.	Price Each	Wheels	Tires	Packed	Weight Per Crate
9		8 and 12-in.	½-in. Rubber	One in Crate	55 lbs.

The Genuine Irish Mail sells better than all other hand cars.

Built like the Irish Mail with bed on rear. Encourages children to run errands because it is fun. Bed for carrying parcels or a convenient riding place for small children.

THE IRISH MAIL LINE

BEN HUR RACER
Two Sizes

No.	Price Each	Wheels	Tires	Packed	Weight Per Crate
20		12 inch	½-in. Rubber	One in Crate	50 lbs.
21		14 inch	⅝-in. Rubber	One in Crate	55 lbs.
Irish Mail developed boys and girls make better men and women.					

Constructed along automobile lines.
Drop frame, tilted seat, extra wheel.
Long, low, racy and easy to run.

GREEN DRAGON
For Boys and Girls

No.	Price Each	Wheels	Tires	Packed	Weight Per Crate
29		12-inch	⅝-in. Rubber	One in Crate	46 lbs.
The Irish Mail sells itself.					

A new handcar with automobile front
axle and steering knuckles. Heavy
wheels and tires, strong, well made,
very attractive.

THE IRISH MAIL LINE

No. 1. AUTOMOBILE. Price Each $...............

Packed One in Crate. Shipping weight 90 lbs.

Body 15x45 inches; racer design; crank drive; concealed gears; 10-inch tubular steel steering wheel; genuine automobile steering knuckles; 12x½-inch rubber tired wheels.

Finish: Body, royal blue with gray wheels; or body black with red wheels.

BI-KAR

No.	Price Each	Wheels	Tires	Packed	Weight Per Crate
31		14 inch	¾-in. Rubber	One in Crate	70 lbs.
The Irish Mail is used in every civilized country in the world.					

A two-wheel handcar with side car, similar to a motorcycle. Side car can be detached.

THE IRISH MAIL LINE

No. 14.   AUTOMOBILE.   Roller Bearing.   Price Each $...............
Body 13x46-in., chrome yellow. Radiator front black. Decorated in gold bronze
striped in black. Inside self-starter. Nickel-plated trimmings on radiator an
bonnet. Tinned steering rod. Nickel-plated steering wheel and hub caps. U
holstered seat and back. Knuckle-joint Auto gear, black enameled. Bumpe
12x½-in. rubber-tired wheels, roller-bearing, yellow enameled.
Packed one in crate; weight per crate, 65 lbs.
Lamps and horn extra. For ⅝-in. rubber tires see price list.

No. 15.   AUTOMOBILE.   Roller-Bearing   Price Each...............
Body 14½x41½ in., Auto red, striped with white. Decorated in gold bronze.
Upholstered seat. Inside self-starter. Nickel-plated trimmings on bonnet and
radiator. Nickel-plated hub caps. Nickel-plated steering wheel. Tinned steer-
ing rod. Knuckle-joint Auto gear and fenders, black enameled. Bumper. 14x
½ in. rubber-tired wheels, roller bearing, black enameled.
Packed one in crate; weight per crate, 75 lbs.
Lamps and horn extra. For ⅝-in. rubber tires see price list.

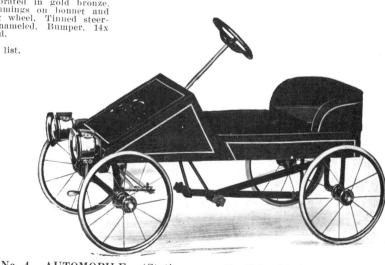

No. 4.   AUTOMOBILE.   (Stationary seat)—Price Each $...............
No. 5.   AUTOMOBILE.   (Adjustable seat)—Price Each $...............
Body 12x28 in., chrome green, striped in white.
Decorated in gold bronze. Black steering rod. Starting crank.
Knuckle-joint gear and steering wheel, black enameled.
10x3-8 in. rubber-tired wheels, black enameled. No. 4 has 10x3-8 wheels.
No. 5 has 12x3-8 wheels.
Packed one in crate; weight per crate: No. 4, 30 lbs.; No. 5, 45 lbs.
Lamps and horn extra. For ½-in. rubber tires see price list.

No. 7.   AUTOMOBILE.   Price Each $...............
Body 13x32 in., chrome yellow, striped in black. Decorated in black. Tinned
steering rod. Starting crank. Knuckle-joint gear and steering wheel, black
enameled. 12x3-8 in., rubber-tired wheels, black enameled. Bumper.
Packed one in crate; weight per crate, 40 lbs.
Lamps and horn extra.   For ½-in. rubber tires see price list.

No. 8.   AUTOMOBILE   **Price Each $**...............
No. 9.   AUTOMOBILE, (larger size)   **Price Each $**...............
No. 8, Body 13x32 in.; No. 9, Body, 14½x38 in., chrome green, nicely striped.
Decorated in gold bronze. Nickel-plated trimmings on bonnet. Tinned steering
rod. Black enameled steering wheel. Knuckle-joint Auto gear, black enameled.
No. 8 has 12x3-8 in. rubber-tired wheels and No. 9 has 14x3-8 rubber-tired
wheels, red enameled. Inside self-starter. Bumper.
Packed one in crate; weight per crate: No. 8, 40 lbs.; No. 9, 50 lbs.
Lamps and horn extra.   For ½-in. rubber tires see price list.

No. 2.   AUTOMOBILE.   Price Each $...............

Packed One in Crate.   Shipping weight 90 lbs.

Body 15x45 inches; racer design; crank drive; concealed gears; 10-inch
tubular steel steering wheel; genuine automobile steering knuckles;
12x½-inch rubber tired wheels.
Finish: Body, red with green wheels; or body yellow with black wheels.

THE IRISH MAIL LINE

No. 12.   AUTOMOBILE.   Price Each $...............

Body 13x44½ in., Milori green, striped in lemon yellow. Decorated in lemon yellow. Tinned steering rod. Starting crank. Knuckle-joint Auto gear and steering wheel, black enameled. 12x½-in. Rubber-tired wheels, red enameled. Bumper. Gas tank.
Packed one in crate; weight per crate, 60 lbs.
Lamps and horn extra. For ⅝-in. rubber tires see price list.

No. 13.   AUTOMOBILE   Price Each $...............

Body 14½x40 in., Cobalt blue, striped in gold bronze. Decorated in gold bronze. Inside self-starter. Tinned steering rod. Nickel-plated trimmings on radiator and bonnet. Black enameled steering wheel. Knuckle-joint Auto gear, black enameled. Bumper. 14x½-in. rubber-tired wheels, gray enameled. Nickel-plated hub caps.
Packed one in crate; weight per crate, 55 lbs.
Lamps and horn extra. For ⅝-in. rubber tires see price list.

No. 6.....AUTOMOBILE.   Price Each $...............

Body 12x28 in., chrome green, striped in white. Decorated in gold bronze. Black steering rod. Starting crank. Knuckle-joint gear and steering wheel, black enameled. 10x3-8 in. rubber-tired wheels, black enameled.
Packed one in crate; weight per crate, 30 lbs.
Lamps and horn extra. For ½-in. rubber tires see price list.

THE IRISH MAIL LINE

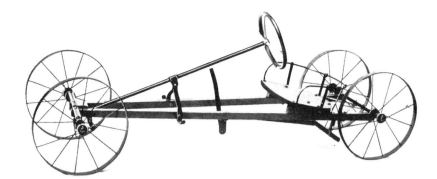

No. 50. **CALIFORNIA COASTER** Price Each $ ....
Packed one in crate, shipping weight 55 lbs.

THE "SAFETY FIRST COASTER": Built with drop frame so rider sits eight inches from ground; automobile steering knuckles with rings for attaching rope; 10-inch indestructible tubular steel steering wheel; reliable brake; convenient foot rest; 9-16 inch axles; extra strong 14-inch steel wheels; wheel base 49 inches, tread 17 inches; hickory frame; tilted seat, 11x14 inches with steel railing.

FINISH: Frame pea green; seat red; steering wheel, brake and axles black.

No. 52. CALIFORNIA COASTER. Price Each $ ....
Packed one in crate, shipping weight 60 lbs.

Modernized construction. Notice the slant to steering wheel. Automobile steering knuckles with rings for attaching rope; 10-inch indestructible tubular steel steering wheel; wood bolsters with 9-16 inch steel axle; seat 10x52 inches with rounded edge; reliable brake; convenient foot rest; extra strong 14-inch steel wheels; wheel base, 46 inches; tread, 17 inches; seat, 13 inches from ground.

FINISH: Seat pea green; wheels, red; steering wheel, brake and axles, black.

NANCY HANKS and BLACK BEAUTY

No. 19. **NANCY HANKS.** Price Each $ ....
Packed one in a crate. Shipping weight, 32 pounds.
Steel sulky. Pedal drive. Heavy 8 and 12 in. steel wheel with ½-inch rubber tires. Wood horse with metal legs, real hair mane and tail. Painted, horse gloss black, sulky green, wheels red. Dimensions, horse 15 in. x 22 in., horse and sulky 19 in. x 45 in.

Pioneer Aeroplanes

In a recent survey made by a leading weekly magazine to determine the popular hero with the American boy, Colonel Chas. A. Lindbergh won by an overwhelming majority. The new "Pioneer" *Spirit of St. Louis* holds the same place of popularity in the Children's Vehicle field.

This new number is an exact replica of the famous "Old Bus" and does everything but fly. All metal except the rudder and propeller. Finished in the famous silver bronze. Equipped with heavy balloon type aeroplane wheels. Number 16 has a high-speed gear drive. Number 14 has the regular Gendron treadle drive.

Three other planes complete the Pioneer line. No. 12, also called the *Spirit of St. Louis* is a wood plane with wings that move with the action of the front wheels. No. 10, called *Columbia* has stationary wings. No. 8 is a small model for the little folks and carries the insignia, *Scout.*

No. 16
Spirit of St. Louis
(Name Copyrighted)

The Gendron "Pioneer Line" Vehicles for Children

— SOLD BY —

Reiss Merc. Co.
MOBILE, ALA.

Form 105 Printed in U. S. A.

Pioneer Automobiles

Equipped with all the new accessories. Finished in the new bright tints and shades. Designed after the very latest models in the automobile field. The last word in styles and equipment.

Roadsters	Patrols
Speedsters	Fire Chief Speeders
Racemobiles	Hose Carts
Dump Trucks	Ladder Trucks
Fire Trucks	Locomotive
Speed Boat	Auto Bike

Electric Motor Driven Sport Roadster

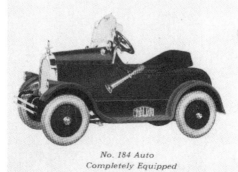

No. 184 Auto
Completely Equipped

PLYMOUTH AUTO

Model No. 570
Electric Lights
(For Children 3 to 6 Years)

OVERALL DIMENSIONS: Length 43", Width 21".
WHEELS: 10" Roller bearing wheels with ¾" rubber tires. Wheels are Artillery type with large hub caps.
EQUIPMENT: Most modern streamline body, with wide streamline fenders. Latest "V" type sloping radiator, spring type chassis, electric lamps mounted on fenders, adjustable rubber pedals, running boards, seat pad, streamline windshield, French bulb horn, bumper.
FINISH: Body is finished in Black baked enamel, with Green striping. Fenders and running boards in Green. Wheels Artillery type in Green and Silver.
PACKED: One in a carton, K. D. Construction makes set-up easy.
SHIPPING WEIGHT: 48 lbs.

FORD AUTO

Model No. 5701
(For Children 3 to 6 Years)
Equipped with Electric Headlights

OVERALL DIMENSIONS: Length 43", Width 21".
WHEELS: 10" Roller bearing wheels with ¾" rubber tires. Wheels are with large hub caps.
EQUIPMENT: Most modern streamline body, with wide streamline fenders. Latest "V" type sloping radiator, spring type chassis, electric lamps mounted on fenders, adjustable rubber pedals, running boards, seat pad, streamline windshield. French bulb horn, bumper and electric lights.
FINISH: Body is finished in Ivory baked enamel, with Red panels. Fenders and running boards in Red. Wheels in Ivory with Red stripe. Radiator in Silver.
PACKED: One in a carton K. D. Construction makes set-up easy.
SHIPPING WEIGHT: 48 lbs.

NOTE: Automobiles with electric lights are furnished with bulbs, wiring, battery holders and switch. No batteries are furnished. Two standard flashlight cells are required to operate lights.

2½ TON MACK DUMP TRUCK

Model No. 671
(For Children 3 to 7 years)
Equipped with Electric Lights

This Steelcraft Juvenile Mack Dump Truck is not just a fragile toy for Children, it is a real truck, carefully designed and carefully built of heavy gauge automobile steel. It operates easily, carries heavy loads, and stands up under the hard usage the child will put upon it.

This Steelcraft Juvenile Mack Dump Truck resembles in detail the large Mack Trucks seen daily on the streets. It has real carbon steel springs, adjustable pedals, roller bearing wheels, ball bearings on rear axle, patented dumping mechanism, heavy double crowned steel fenders, French bulb horn, gear shift lever, spotlight, dump body with tail gate, electric headlights.

The finish is in baked enamel (not painted on) and will endure. Bumper is chromium plated.

SPECIFICATIONS

OVERALL DIMENSIONS: Length 54″, Width 22½″.

SIZE OF BOX: Length 18½″, Width 14″, Depth 5″.

WHEELS: 10″ Balloon type, artillery style with large hub caps and ¾″ rubber tires.

ELECTRIC LIGHTS: Equipped with headlights and spotlight, with bulbs.

CAPACITY: 150 lbs.

SHIPPED: One in a crate, for easy assembly. SHIPPING WEIGHT: 85 lbs.

FINISH: Hood, seat and box Red. Chassis Black. Wheels Aluminum with Red spokes. Green panels on hood.

PNEUMATIC TIRED
2½ TON MACK DUMP TRUCK
Model No. 670

This item is exactly the same as the Dump Truck illustrated and described above except the wheels will be Ball Bearing type with 2¾″ Pneumatic Tires.

LINCOLN

Model No. 640

Pneumatic Tire Equipped

Equipped with Electric Headlights, Spotlight and Tail Light, with Bright and Dim Switch and Electric Horn

OVERALL DIMENSIONS: Length 53", Width 21".

WHEELS: 10" ball bearing wheels with 2¾" Pneumatic Tires and large chromium plated hub caps.

EQUIPMENT INCLUDES: Streamline body, chromium plated "V" type radiator, latest design. Other equipment includes: latest style one-piece streamline fenders with skirts, ball bearing spring type chassis, running board spotlight, chromium plated radiator cap, chromium plated lamps. Electric Horn, ball top hand brake, dummy top, chromium plated tubular bumper, chromium plated steering wheel, dummy fender lights, adjustable windshield, beauty wings, folding trunk rack and tail light on rear, two rear vision mirrors. Headlights, running board spotlight and tail light are equipped with electric light bulbs.

FINISH: Body in Red with Ivory panels, Fenders and running boards in black with De Luxe striping and panelling.

PACKED: One in a crate for easy setup.

SHIPPING WEIGHT: 90 lbs.

NOTE: *Service on pneumatic tires is obtainable at all Goodyear branches and dealers.*

ALL STEEL MONOPLANE

2¾″ Pneumatic Tires

Model No. 695

(Propeller revolves when Plane is in motion)
Equipped with electric landing light

In this Aeroplane, the design and lines of a large monoplane have been carried out as closely as possible. It is built entirely of heavy gauge steel.

SPECIFICATIONS

OVERALL DIMENSIONS: Length 53½″, Height 27½″, Wing spread 30″.
FINISH: Body in Maroon, Ivory striped. Wing and tailpieces Ivory. Bullseye on wheels Ivory. Landing gear black enamel.
EQUIPMENT: As shown, includes imitation motor, chrome plated propeller, electric landing light and dummy tail light.
WHEELS: Front 10″, contained ball bearing with 2¾″ pneumatic tires. Rear 8½″ double disc, with ⅝″ rubber tires, artillery spokes.
PACKING: One in a crate. SHIPPING WEIGHT: 71 lbs.

AIR MAIL

Model No. 698

(For Children 2 to 4 Years)

SPECIFICATIONS

FINISH: Body and wheels in Red baked enamel. Wings, tailpieces and propeller in Ivory baked enamel, attractively striped.
OVERALL DIMENSIONS: Length 41″, Width 30″.
WHEELS: Front 8½″ with ⅝″ tire. Skid wheels 6¾″ with ⅝″ tire. Front axle in ball bearing suspension. Wheels with artillery spokes.
PACKED: One in a carton, K. D. SHIPPING WEIGHT: 30 lbs.

Model No. 699

Exactly same as No. 698 above except will have 10″ front wheels with 2¾″ Goodyear Pneumatic Tires.

THE ARMY SCOUT PLANE

Model No. 696

Equipped with electric landing light
(For Children 3 to 7 Years)

This is a popular priced Aeroplane, in an intermediate size. The body, wings, struts, motor, propeller and undergear are all of heavy stamped steel. The design is graceful, the cockpit roomy. It has an electric landing light.

SPECIFICATIONS

FINISH: Body and wheels in Green baked enamel. Wing, tailpieces and pants in Ivory baked enamel. Motor and undergear in Black baked enamel. Propeller chrome plated.
OVERALL DIMENSIONS: Length 46″, Width (Wing spread tip to tip) 30″.
WHEELS: Front 10″, balloon type roller bearings with artillery spokes and large hub caps, ¾″ fancy tread rubber tires. Rear 8½″ double disc with ⅝″ rubber tires—artillery spokes.
PACKED: One in a carton, K. D. SHIPPING WEIGHT: 40 lbs.

Model No. 697

Exactly same as No. 696 above, except will have 10″ front wheels with 2¾″ Goodyear Pneumatic Tires. No pants over front wheels.

2½ TON MACK HOOK AND LADDER

Electric Head and Spotlights
Model No. 690
(For Children 3 to 7 Years)

IT IS mounted on our No. 671 Truck Chassis. Has springs and adjustable rubber pedals and ball bearings on rear axle. It has seats for two children, the driver and a passenger. The equipment, large chrome plated bell with pull cord, electric spotlight, electric headlamps and chromium tubular bumper, lanterns and ladders, gear shift lever, are all of highest quality. The side rails are chromium plated.

SPECIFICATIONS

FINISH: Body in brilliant Red baked enamel. Chassis in Black. Wheels in Aluminum with Red spokes.

OVERALL DIMENSIONS: With ladders—Length 62″, Width 22½″.

OVERALL DIMENSIONS: Without ladders—Length 47½″, Width 22½″.

WHEELS: 10″ balloon type, artillery style, double disc with contained roller bearings and ¾″ fancy tread rubber tires. Wheels have large hub caps.

PACKED: One in a crate. SHIPPING WEIGHT: 90 lbs.
(For easy setup)

NOTE: *Model on this page is equipped with electric headlights with bulbs, wiring and switch, but without batteries. Use two (2) standard flashlight dry cells for this installation.*

Note that overall dimensions on these new type Juvenile Automobiles are overall dimensions of the body. These sizes are not achieved by protruding bumpers or overhanging fenders.

These new style Autos are all car, every inch of them.

13 years ago we revolutionized the Juvenile Automobile Industry when we introduced the first all steel Juvenile Automobile.

The 1936 Steelcraft Models of Automobiles with fenders an integral part of the body are as revolutionary.

There is nothing in the industry to approach them for

    Sales Appeal
    Eye Appeal
      or
    Practicability

Chevrolet Automobile *ste*

Model No. 540
(For Children 2 to 6 Years)

OVERALL DIMENSIONS: Length, 39″; width, 17½″.
WHEELS: 8½″ Double disc, new artillery type with large dome hub caps and ⅝″ rubber tires.
ELECTRIC LIGHTS: Large ornamental lamp bodies are fastened to side of car, equipped with bulbs, lens, wiring and switch. (Two batteries required, not furnished.)
EQUIPMENT: Windshield, bulb horn, bumper, seat pad, adjustable pedals, motometer.
FENDERS: Front and rear are an integral part of the body.
FINISH: Maroon with light Ivory trim.
PACKING: One to a carton. WEIGHT: 37 lbs.
Special construction reduces set-up work to minimum.

Chevrolet Chief Automobile

Model No. 545
(For Children 2 to 6 Years)

OVERALL DIMENSIONS: Length, 39″; width, 17½″.
WHEELS: 8½″ Double disc, new artillery type, with large dome hub caps and ⅝″ rubber tires.
ELECTRIC LIGHTS: Large ornamental lamp bodies are fastened to side of car, equipped with bulbs, lens, wiring and switch. (Two batteries required, not furnished.)
EQUIPMENT: Large chromium plated Fire Chief bell, bumper, seat pad, adjustable pedals.
FENDERS: Front and rear are an integral part of the body.
FINISH: White with Red trim. All baked enamels.
PACKING: One to a carton. WEIGHT: 37 lbs.
Special construction reduces set-up work to minimum.

STUDEBAKER CHIEF AUTO

Model No. 5713

Pneumatic Tire Equipped   **Electric Lights**   (For Children 3 to 6 Years)

OVERALL DIMENSIONS: Length 43", Width 21".

WHEELS: 10" Ball Bearing with 2¾" Pneumatic Tires.

EQUIPMENT: Modern streamline body with wide streamline fenders and running boards. Latest "V" type sloping radiator, spring type chassis, adjustable rubber pedals, seat pad, bumper, Fire Chief bell and decorations on body. Electric lights mounted on fenders.

FINISH: Body in White baked enamel. Fenders, running boards and panels on body, in Red.

PACKED: One in a carton, K. D. Construction makes set-up easy.   SHIPPING WEIGHT: 51 lbs.

BUYERS: This model will be equipped with chromium plated radiator, and Artillery type wheels not shown on illustration.

BUICK

Model No. 610

Equipped with Electric Lights   (For Children 3 to 7 Years)

OVERALL DIMENSIONS: Length 47" Width 21".

WHEELS: 10" balloon type with ¾" fancy tread rubber tires. Artillery Wheels with large bright hub caps.

EQUIPMENT: 1934 type streamline body and streamline "V" type radiator—fenders are also streamline of latest design with skirts. Has spring type ball bearing chassis, adjustable rubber pedals, ball bearing pull straps, one-piece streamline fenders with running boards and running board splashers, seat pad, radiator chrome plated, electric lighted headlamps, steering wheel, French bulb horn, running board spotlight, folding trunk rack, ball top hand brake, cadmium plated tubular bumper, cast radiator cap, dummy fender lights and dummy top.

FINISH: Body in Ivory with Red panels on hood and Red splashers. Red fenders and running boards. Black trunk rack. Wheels in Silver with Red spokes.

PACKED: One in a crate. For easy setup.

SHIPPING WEIGHT: 87 lbs.

Model No. 612

Same as above except packed in a carton K. D. Design makes setup work easy.

SHIPPING WEIGHT: 69 lbs. Packed one in a carton.

CHRYSLER IMPERIAL AIRFLOW

De Luxe Equipped
2¾″ Pneumatic Tired
Model No. 581
(For Children 3 to 8 Years)

SPECIFICATIONS

OVERALL DIMENSIONS: Length 43¾″, Width 18″.

WHEELS: 10″ ball bearing, with 2¾″ pneumatic tires.

EQUIPMENT: Very realistic Air Flow designed body of 20 gauge Automobile body steel. Chassis spring type ball bearing. The fenders are an integral part of the body. Other equipment includes rubber adjustable pedals, windshield, electric headlights, electric spotlight on hood, French bulb horn, ball top hand brake, designed instrument board, radiator ornament-Chrysler design. The striping and designs are special Chrysler type.

FINISH: Body in Green baked enamel. Shutter of radiator Ivory, Chrysler type louvers on side in Ivory. Ornaments on rear fenders in Ivory. Bumper, headlamps and windshield in Silver.

PACKING: One to a carton K. D. SHIPPING WEIGHT: 53 lbs.

Special construction reduces setup labor to a minimum

NOTE: *This Auto is furnished with electric light bulbs, wiring, battery holder and switch—no batteries are furnished. Two standard flashlight cells are required to operate lights.*

Electric Lights
Artillery Wheels
Springs
Ball Bearings
Windshield
Bulb Horn
Bumper

Plymouth Auto

Model No. 570
Electric Lights
(For Children 3 to 6 Years)

OVERALL DIMENSIONS: Length, 43″; width, 21″.
WHEELS: 10″ Roller bearing wheels with ¾″ rubber tires. Wheels are artillery type with large dome hub caps.
EQUIPMENT: Most modern streamline body, with wide streamline fenders. Latest "V" type sloping radiator, spring type chassis, electric lamps mounted on fenders, adjustable rubber pedals, running boards, seat pad, streamline windshield, French bulb horn, bumper.
FINISH: Body is finished in Green baked enamel, with Ivory striping. Fenders and running boards in Black. Wheels artillery type in Green with Ivory Stripe.
PACKED: One in a carton, K. D. Construction makes set-up easy.
SHIPPING WEIGHT: 48 lbs.

Electric Lights
Artillery Wheels
Springs
Ball Bearings
Fire Chief Bell

Dodge Chief

Model No. 571
Electric Lights
(For Children 3 to 6 Years)

OVERALL DIMENSIONS: Length, 43″; width, 21″.
WHEELS: 10″ Roller bearing artillery wheels with ¾″ rubber tires. Wheels are with large dome hub caps.
EQUIPMENT: Modern streamline body with wide streamline fenders and running boards. Latest "V" type sloping radiator, spring type chassis, adjustable rubber pedals, seat pad, bumper, Fire Chief bell and decorations on body. Electric lights mounted on fenders.
FINISH: Body in White baked enamel. Fenders, running boards and panels on body, in Red. Wheels, Red, with White stripe.
PACKED: One in a carton, K. D. Construction makes set-up easy.
SHIPPING WEIGHT: 51 lbs.
NOTE: Automobiles with electric lights are furnished with bulbs, wiring, battery holder and switch. No batteries are furnished. Two standard flashlight cells required to operate.

1935 Catalog Page

PONTIAC CHIEF AUTO—DeLUXE

Model No. 535
Equipped with Electric Headlights
(For Children 2 to 5 years)

SPECIFICATIONS

OVERALL DIMENSIONS: Length 38″, Width 18½″.

WHEELS: 8½″ diameter double steel disc wheels with ⅝″ rubber tires. Wheels are artillery type design with large hub caps.

EQUIPMENT: New streamline body, adjustable rubber pedals, ball bearing pedal rods, one piece streamline fenders and running boards, new racing type bullet type headlamps, equipped with electric lights, Pontiac type beading running from cowl to bottom of radiator, front bumper, Fire Chief bell and pull cord, steering wheel.

FINISH: Body in Red with Silver striping. Radiator lamp bodies and bumper in Silver. Chief design in Ivory panel. Bell bracket in Silver. Wheels in Silver with Red spokes.

PACKING: One to a carton K. D. SHIPPING WEIGHT: 43 lbs.

DODGE CHIEF

Model No. 571
Electric Lights
(For Children 1½ to 4 Years)

OVERALL DIMENSIONS: Length 43″, Width 21″.

WHEELS: 10″ Roller bearing wheels with ¾″ rubber tires. Wheels are with large hub caps.

EQUIPMENT: Modern streamline body with wide streamline fenders and running boards. Latest "V" type sloping radiator, spring type chassis, adjustable rubber pedals, seat pad, bumper, Fire Chief bell and decorations on body. Electric lights mounted on fenders.

FINISH: Body in White baked enamel. Fenders, running boards and panels on body, in Red. Wheels Red, with white stripe.

PACKED: One in a carton K. D. Construction makes set-up easy.

SHIPPING WEIGHT: 51 lbs.

NOTE: Automobiles with electric lights are furnished with bulbs, wiring, battery holder and switch. No batteries are furnished. Two standard flashlight cells required to operate.

CHRYSLER AIR FLOW

Model No. 580
Equipped with Electric Headlamps
(For Children 3 to 8 Years)

NOTHING that we, as manufacturers, have ever produced, has afforded us the satisfaction that we have derived from knowing that in this Automobile we have practically reached the ultimate in what can be offered the public at moderate price in a pedal propelled Juvenile Auto. The hood is designed to resemble in detail the hood of the regular 1935 Chrysler Air Flow. The fenders are an integral part of the body, thus eliminating the greatest part of setup costs, and the annoyance caused by fenders coming loose. The body is large and roomy—the auto is easy running and built of 20 gauge Automobile Body Steel, will stand the hardest use. Only specialists in sheet metal stampings would produce an Auto like this one.

SPECIFICATIONS

OVERALL DIMENSIONS: Length 43¾″, Width 18″.

WHEELS: 10″ roller bearing, heavy double disc type with ¾″ rubber tires and large hub caps.

EQUIPMENT: Electric headlamps—Air Flow design. French bulb horn, front bumper, windshield, ball bearing spring type chassis, adjustable rubber pedals, Chrysler radiator ornament and steering wheel. The fenders and running boards are part of the body.

FINISH: Body in Red. Radiator panel and striping on body in Ivory. Wheels in Red with Ivory stripe. Bumper, windshield and lamp bodies finished in Silver.

PACKING: One to carton. SHIPPING WEIGHT: 50 lbs. The construction of this Auto reduces setup work to a minimum.

NOTE: This auto is furnished with electric light bulbs, wiring, battery holder and switch. No batteries are furnished. Two standard flashlight cells are required to operate lights.

CHEVROLET AUTO

Model No. 572

Equipped with Electric Headlamps

(For Children 3 to 7 Years)

OVERALL DIMENSIONS: Length 46″, Width 21″.

WHEELS: 10″ Balloon style, artillery type, with large hub caps and ¾″ rubber tires.

EQUIPMENT: Streamline body with wide streamline fenders and running boards. Modern Radiator, ball bearing spring type chassis, adjustable rubber pedals, designed instrument board, hand-brake with ball top, French bulb horn. Electric bullet type headlamps, electric running board spotlight. Cadmium plated bumper, luggage rack, racing type windshield.

FINISH: Body in Grey. Fenders and running boards in Black. Side panels in Red. Body striping in Red. Wheels Silver with Red spokes. Radiator shutter, windshield and headlamps finished in Silver.

PACKING: One to carton K. D. SHIPPING WEIGHT: 56 lbs.

SPORT ROADSTER

Model No. 510

Equipped with Electric Lights

(For Children 2 to 5 years)

OVERALL DIMENSIONS: Length 37″. Width 16½″.

WHEELS: Double disc 8″, with ⅝″ Rubber tires.

HEADLIGHTS: Equipped with electric headlights with lens.

FENDERS: Large size streamlined fenders over all four wheels—Pontoon type.

FINISH: Body in Red baked enamel with latest design Ivory striping. Fenders in Ivory with Red striping.

PACKED: One to a carton K. D. SHIPPING WEIGHT: 26 lbs.

ACE AUTO

Model No. 500

For Children 1½ to 4 Years

SPECIFICATIONS

OVERALL DIMENSIONS: Length 31¼″, Width 15½″.

FINISH: Body in Red. Wheels in Ivory striped in Red. Under-gear in Red. All in baked enamel.

WHEELS: 8¼″ double steel disc with ½″ rubber tires.

SHIPPED: One in a carton K. D. SHIPPING WEIGHT: 21 lbs.

Model No. 501

ACE AUTO

This model is exactly the same as the one above, except will have bullet type electric headlamps.

CHIEF AUTO

Model No. 506

Equipped with Electric Lights

(For Children 1½ to 4 years)

SPECIFICATIONS

OVERALL DIMENSIONS: Length 31¼″, Width 15½″.

EQUIPMENT: Electric Lights—Fire Chief Bell.

WHEELS: 8¼″ double disc with ⅝″ rubber tires. Artillery design large hub caps.

FINISH: Body and seat in Red with attractive striping in Ivory. Wheels in Silver with Red spokes.

SHIPPED: One in a carton K. D. SHIPPING WEIGHT: 24 lbs.

NOTE: Automobiles with electric lights are furnished with bulbs, wiring, battery holders and switch.
No batteries are furnished, two standard flashlight cells being required to operate.

PONTIAC AUTO
Model No. 530
Equipped with Electric Headlights   (For Children 2 to 5 years)
SPECIFICATIONS
Modern, realistic in design, and beautiful in finish—this auto will be a treat for its proud owner.
OVERALL DIMENSIONS: Length 38″, Width 18½″.
WHEELS: 8½″ diameter double disc steel wheels with ⅝″ rubber tires. Wheels are artillery type design with large hub caps.
EQUIPMENT: New streamline body, adjustable rubber pedals, ball bearing pull straps, new one-piece streamline type fenders and running board, racing type windshield, new bullet type headlights equipped with electric lights, Pontiac type beading running from cowl to bottom of radiator, Pontiac style radiator ornament, bulb horn, front bumper and steering wheel.
FINISH: Body in Black with Pontiac style striping and louvers in Silver. Fenders, running boards and undergear in Green. Lamps, bumpers and windshield frame in Silver. Wheels in Silver with Green spokes.
PACKING: One to carton K. D. SHIPPING WEIGHT: 43 lbs.   (Construction makes setup easy).

NASH
Model No. 560
Equipped with Electric Headlights   (For Children 2 to 5 years)
OVERALL DIMENSIONS: Length 37″, Width 18½″.
WHEELS: Double disc, 8½″ with ⅝″ rubber tires, with large hub caps.
EQUIPMENT: Includes new streamline body, adjustable rubber pedals, ball bearing pull straps, one piece streamlined new type fenders and running boards, new type racing windshield, bullet type headlamps equipped with electric lights, radiator ornament, horn, front bumper, steering wheel and deck on rear.
FINISH: Body in Light Brown, with Dark Brown striping and panels. Fenders and running boards in Dark Brown. Wheels in Ivory with Dark Brown stripe. Radiator shutter sprayed Silver.
PACKED: One in a carton K. D. (New construction makes setup work very easy.) SHIPPING WEIGHT: 38 lbs.

PONTIAC CHIEF AUTO
Model No. 525
Equipped with Electric Headlamps   (For Children 2 to 5 years)

OVERALL DIMENSIONS: Length 33″, Width 18¼″.

WHEELS: 8½″ diameter, double disc steel wheels with ⅝″ rubber tires. Wheels are equipped with extra large hub caps.

EQUIPMENT: Fire Chief Bell, Electric Headlamps, Front Bumper, Rubber Pedals, Steering Wheel. The Hood is decorated with Fire Chief insignia.

FINISH: Red body—Shutter of Radiator in Silver, beads on hood in Silver. The bumper finished in Silver. Pontiac type louvers on side. Wheels Red with Ivory stripe.

PACKING: One to a carton, K. D. SHIPPING WEIGHT: 30 lbs.

ESSEX AUTO
Model No. 515
Equipped with Electric Headlights   (For Children 2 to 5 years)

OVERALL DIMENSIONS: Length 33″, Width 18¼″.

WHEELS: 8½″ diameter, double disc with ⅝″ tires. Wheels have extra large hub caps.

EQUIPMENT: Rubber pedals, front bumper, steering wheel, radiator ornament, horn, windshield, and electric headlamps.

FINISH: Body in Green, with Ivory panels and striping. Green wheels with Ivory stripe. Radiator shutter in silver. All are hard baked enamels.

PACKING: One to carton, K. D. SHIPPING WEIGHT: 30 lbs.

1-TON MACK DUMP TRUCK

Model No. 652
(For Children 3 to 6 Years)

SPECIFICATIONS

FINISH: Box, hood, seat in Red and wheels in Red. Hood striped attractively in Ivory.
OVERALL DIMENSIONS: Length 45″, Width 20″.
SIZE OF BOX: Length 15″, Width 14″, Depth 5″.
WHEELS: 8½″ double disc with ⅝″ rubber tires.
CAPACITY: 100 lbs.
EQUIPMENT: Chassis—spring type, rubber pedals.
PACKED: One in a carton K. D. SHIPPING WEIGHT: 37 lbs.

1-TON MACK HOOK AND LADDER

Electric Headlights
Model No. 680
(For Children 3 to 6 Years)

This is a real two-seater, pedal propelled Fire Truck for the small child. It has springs, ball bearing pedal straps, adjustable rubber pedals, gear shift lever, large chrome plated bell, with pull cord, electric headlights, ladders and lanterns.

SPECIFICATIONS

FINISH: Body and hood in Red baked enamel.
OVERALL DIMENSIONS: With ladders—length 50½″, Width 20″.
OVERALL DIMENSIONS: Without ladders—Length 40¾″, Width 20″.
LENGTH OF LADDERS: (2)—27″ each.
WHEELS: 8″ double disc with ⅝″ rubber tires, with large hub caps.
PACKED: One in a carton, K. D. SHIPPING WEIGHT: 42 lbs.

NOTE: *No. 680 Truck above is equipped with electric lights, with bulbs, wiring, battery holder and switch. No batteries are furnished. Two standard flashlight cells are required to operate.*

2-TON MACK DUMP TRUCK
Electric Lights
Model No. 662
(For Children 3 to 7 Years)

This model has springs, fenders and running boards. French bulb horn, electric lights, hand brake, adjustable rubber pedals and will carry a load up to 150 pounds. The construction of the truck, all of heavy gauge steel with heavy steel wheels, is a guarantee of long life.

SPECIFICATIONS
FINISH: Hood and seat Ivory. Box and fenders Dark Brown. Chassis and undergear in Ivory. All in baked enamel.
WHEELS: Silver with Dark Brown spokes. Bumper and lights in Silver.
OVERALL DIMENSIONS: Length 47¾", Width 20".
SIZE OF BOX: Length 15", Width 14", Depth 5".
WHEELS: 10" double disc, artillery type, roller bearing with ¾" fancy tread rubber tires and large hub caps.
EQUIPMENT: Fenders, with running boards, gear shift lever, bumper, French bulb horn and electric headlamps.
CAPACITY: 150 lbs.   PACKED: One in a carton K. D. SHIPPING WEIGHT: 48 lbs.

2-TON MACK DUMP TRUCK
Equipped with 2¾" Pneumatic Tires   Electric Headlamps
Model No. 663
(For Children 3 to 7 Years)
·SPECIFICATIONS

FINISH: Hood and seat Light Brown. Box and fenders Dark Brown. Chassis and undergear in Light Brown—all in baked enamel. Bumper and lights Silver.
OVERALL DIMENSIONS: Length 47¾", Width 20".
SIZE OF BOX: Length 15", Width 14", Depth 5".
WHEELS: 10" double disc ball bearing with 2¾" Pneumatic Tires and large hub caps.
EQUIPMENT: Fenders, with running boards, gear shift lever, bumper, French bulb horn and electric headlamps.
CAPACITY: 150 lbs.   PACKED: One in a carton K. D. SHIPPING WEIGHT: 48 lbs.

NOTE: *The above trucks are equipped with electric lights. Bulbs, wiring, battery holder and switch are furnished. No batteries are furnished. Two standard flashlight cells are required to operate lights.*

DISTINCTIVE FEATURES
On Blue Streak Automobiles

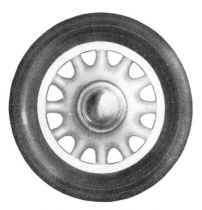

New Steering Wheel and Control Switch

Electric head lights on Blue Streak automobiles are controlled from the modern steering wheel with a simple and trouble-proof switch.

Automobile Wheel

This new wheel used on many 1935 Blue Streak automobiles closely follows the trend in modern automobile design.

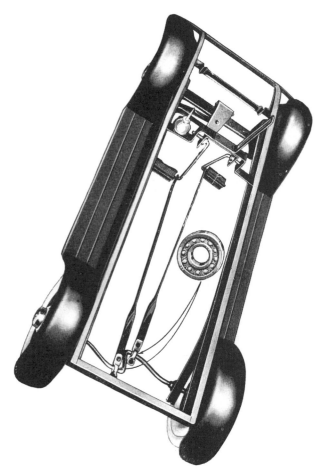

A real electric horn

Several Blue Streak autos include this new and important feature as standard equipment for 1935. Available as an extra accessory on other models at low cost.

Siren

This high speed siren is regular equipment on nearly all fire department models. It produces a shrill shriek in typical Fire Chief fashion.

Ball Bearing Propelling Gear

Blue Streak automobiles propel easily because high grade ball bearings are used at the vital points. This ball bearing construction reduces friction so that the automobiles operate with a minimum amount of effort. The rear axles are cadmium plated and not enameled for further ease of operation.

New Design Radiator Front

Blue Streak automobiles, in pace with 1935 automotive trends, feature this style radiator front on several models.

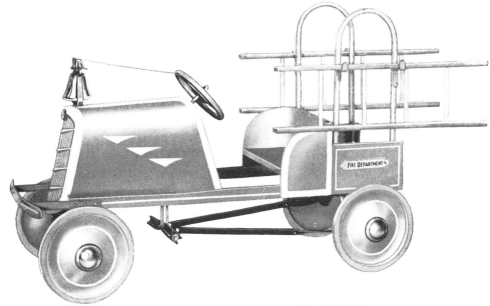

No. 1565 HOOK AND LADDER

Length Overall—44 inches.

Finish—Red, trimmed with white. Red wheels.

Equipment—As shown.

Gear—Ball bearing. Adjustable rubber pedals.

Wheels—9½-inch disc wheels. ⅝-inch rubber tires.

Packing—For easy assembly. Weight per crate, 55 lbs.

No. 1564 HOOK AND LADDER

Same as No. 1565 described above, except packed K. D., one in carton. Weight per carton, 50 lbs.

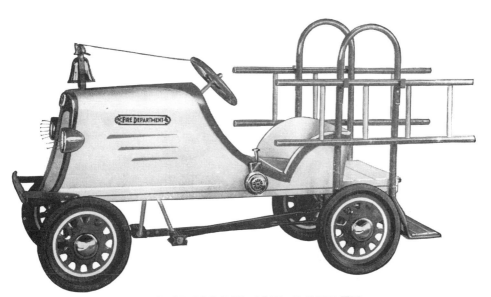

No. 1567 HOOK AND LADDER

Length Overall—49 inches.

Finish—White enamel, trimmed with green and red. Red wheels.

Equipment—As shown, including electric head lights and instrument board.

Gear—Ball bearing. Adjustable rubber pedals.

Wheels—9½-inch spoke type disc wheels. ¾-inch rubber tires.

Packing—For easy assembly. Weight per crate, 63 lbs.

No. 1566 HOOK AND LADDER

Same as No. 1567 described above, except packed K. D., one in carton. Weight per carton, 55 lbs.

No. 1561 FIRE CHIEF

Length Overall—45 inches.

Finish—Red, trimmed with white. Fenders and wheels red.

Equipment—As shown.

Gear—Ball bearing. Adjustable rubber pedals.

Wheels—9½-inch spoke type disc wheels. ¾-inch rubber tires.

Packing—For easy assembly. Weight per crate, 63 lbs.

No. 1560 FIRE CHIEF

Same as No. 1561 Fire Chief described above, except packed
K. D., one in carton. Weight per carton, 53 lbs.

No. 1563 FIRE CHIEF

Length Overall—45 inches.

Finish—White enamel, trimmed with green and red. Fenders and wheels red.

Equipment—As shown, including electric head lights and electric spot light on cowl.

Gear—Ball bearing. Adjustable rubber pedals.

Wheels—9½-inch spoke type disc wheels. ¾-inch rubber tires.

Packing—For easy assembly. Weight per crate, 66 lbs.

No. 1573 HOSE CART

Length Overall—65 inches (ladders extending).

Finish—Red, trimmed with yellow. Red wheels.

Equipment—As shown, including electric head lights, spot light and fire siren. Hose with nozzle, rear signal lights and chromium plated steering wheel. Electric horn.

Gear—Ball bearing. Adjustable rubber pedals.

Wheels—12-inch Rolls auto wheels. Roller bearing. 1-inch rubber tires.

Packing—For easy assembly. Weight per crate, 132 lbs.

No. 1575 FIRE TOWER

Length Overall—70 inches (tower extending).

Finish—Red, trimmed with yellow. Red wheels.

Equipment—As shown, including electric head lights, fire siren, spot light, instrument board, upholstered seat and chromium plated steering wheel. Electric horn.

Gear—Ball bearing. Adjustable rubber pedals.

Wheels—12-inch Rolls auto wheels. Roller bearing. 1-inch rubber tires.

Packing—For easy assembly. Weight per crate, 130 lbs.

No. 1569 RADIO CRUISER

Length Overall—50 inches.

Finish—White enamel, with red and green trim. Fenders and wheels green.

Equipment—As shown, including electric head lights and instrument board.

Gear—Ball bearing. Adjustable rubber pedals.

Wheels—Auto spoke steel wheels. Roller bearing. 1½-inch rubber tires.

Packing—For easy assembly. Weight per crate, 70 lbs.

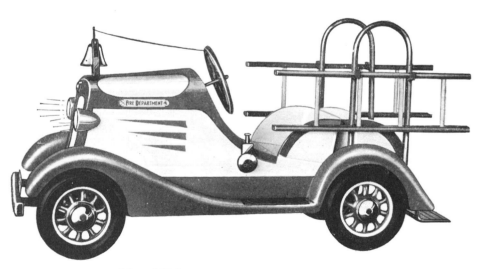

No. 1571 HOOK AND LADDER

Length Overall—52 inches.

Finish—White enamel, with red and green trim. Fenders and wheels red.

Equipment—As shown, including electric head lights and instrument board.

Gear—Ball bearing. Adjustable rubber pedals.

Wheels—Auto spoke steel wheels. Roller bearing. 1½-inch rubber tires.

Packing—For easy assembly. Weight per crate, 73 lbs.

No. 1585 INTERNATIONAL TRUCK

Length Overall—49 inches.

Finish—Red, with black and cream trim. Red fenders and wheels.

Equipment—As shown, including electric head lights and electric spot light on cowl. Rooter horn. Truck style bumper. New style fenders.

Gear—Ball bearing. Adjustable rubber pedals.

Wheels—10-inch disc wheels. 1-inch rubber tires.

Packing—For easy assembly. Weight per crate, 75 lbs.

No. 1584 INTERNATIONAL TRUCK

Same as No. 1585 described above, except packed K. D., one in carton. Weight per carton, 65 lbs.

No. 1587 REPUBLIC TRUCK

Length Overall—55 inches.

Finish—White, with red and green trim. Green fenders and dump box. Red wheels with white stripe.

Equipment—As shown, including electric head lights and electric spot light on cowl. Dump box operated by handle beside driver's seat.

Gear—Ball bearing. Adjustable rubber pedals.

Wheels—10-inch disc wheels. 1-inch rubber tires.

Packing—For easy assembly. Weight per crate, 73 lbs.

No. 1581 WHITE TRUCK

Length Overall—44 inches.

Finish—Jade green, with white and Paradise green trim.

Equipment—As shown, including dump box operated by handle beside driver's seat.

Gear—Adjustable rubber pedals.

Wheels—8-inch disc wheels. ½-inch rubber tires.

Packing—One in carton, K. D. Weight per carton, 39 lbs.

No. 1583 GARFORD TRUCK

Length Overall—48 inches.

Finish—Dark grey, with cream trim. Cream wheels.

Equipment—As shown, including truck style bumper.

Gear—Adjustable rubber pedals.

Wheels—9½-inch disc wheels. ⅝-inch rubber tires.

Packing—For easy assembly. Weight per crate, 55 lbs.

No. 1582 GARFORD TRUCK

Same as No. 1583 described above, except packed K. D., one in carton. Weight per carton, 45 lbs.

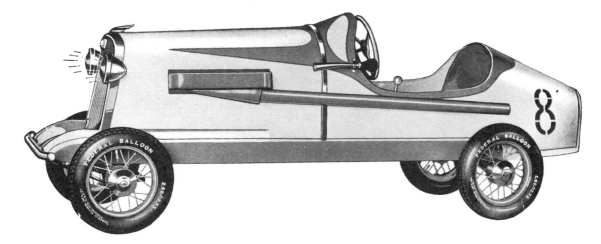

No. 1545 DUESENBERG RACER

Length Overall—70 inches.

Finish—White, trimmed with red.

Equipment—As shown, including electric head lights and instrument board.

Gear—Ball bearing. Adjustable rubber pedals.

Wheels—12-inch ball bearing, nickel plated tangent spoke wire wheels. 2.50″ Federal balloon pneumatic tires.

Packing—For easy assembly. Weight per crate, 100 lbs.

No. 1577 TANDEM

Length Overall—66 inches.

Finish—Red, with black panels and yellow striping, red wheels.

Equipment—As shown, including electric head lights, upholstered seat and instrument board. Chromium plated steering wheel and bumper.

Gear—Ball bearing. Adjustable rubber pedals. Tandem pedal drive.

Wheels—12-inch Rolls auto wheels. Roller bearing. 1-inch rubber tires.

Packing—For easy assembly. Weight per crate, 115 lbs.

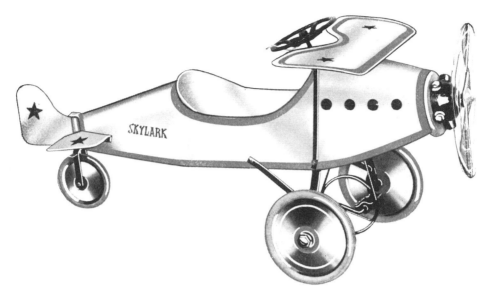

No. 1591 SKYLARK

Length Overall—40 inches. Wing spread, 24 inches.

Finish—Cream, trimmed with red and green.

Equipment—As shown, including revolving propeller.

Wheels—Front, 8-inch disc. $\frac{5}{8}$-inch rubber tires. Rear, 6-inch disc. $\frac{1}{2}$-inch rubber tires.

Packing—One in carton, K. D. Weight per carton, 34 lbs.

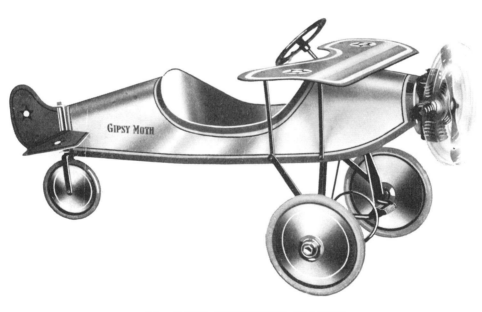

No. 1593 CURTISS HAWK

Length Overall—51 inches. Wing spread, 30 inches.

Finish—Tangerine, trimmed with green and yellow.

Equipment—As shown. Propeller revolves as plane is in motion.

Wheels—Front, 10-inch disc. $\frac{5}{8}$-inch rubber tires. Rear, 7-inch disc. $\frac{1}{2}$-inch rubber tires.

Packing—One in carton, K. D. Weight per carton, 45 lbs.

No. 1501 CHEVROLET

Length Overall—30 inches.

Finish—Cream, trimmed with red. Red wheels.

Equipment—As shown.

Gear—Adjustable rubber pedals.

Wheels—8-inch disc wheels. ½-inch rubber tires.

Packing—One in carton, K. D. Weight per carton, 24 lbs.

No. 1503 FORD

Length Overall—31 inches.

Finish—Red, trimmed with cream. Red wheels.

Equipment—As shown.

Gear—Adjustable rubber pedals.

Wheels—8-inch disc wheels. ½-inch rubber tires.

Packing—One in carton, K. D. Weight per carton, 25 lbs.

No. 1506 PONTIAC

Length Overall—33 inches.

Finish—Light blue, trimmed with cream. Cream wheels.

Equipment—As shown, including electric head lights.

Gear—Adjustable rubber pedals.

Wheels—8-inch disc wheels. ½-inch rubber tires.

Packing—One in carton, K. D. Weight per carton, 27 lbs.

No. 1505 PONTIAC

Same as No. 1506 Pontiac described above, except equipped with non-electric head lights. Weight per carton, 27 lbs.

No. 1511 HUPMOBILE

Length Overall—41 inches.

Finish—Red, trimmed with black and white. Red fenders and wheels.

Equipment—As shown.

Gear—Adjustable rubber pedals.

Wheels—9½-inch disc wheels. ½-inch rubber tires.

Packing—For easy assembly. Weight per crate, 50 lbs.

No. 1510 HUPMOBILE

Same as No. 1511 Hupmobile described above, except packed
K. D., one in carton.   Weight per carton, 40 lbs.

No. 1513 OVERLAND

Length Overall—41 inches.

Finish—Paradise green, trimmed with black and white. Green fenders and wheels.

Equipment—As shown, including electric head lights.

Gear—Adjustable rubber pedals.

Wheels—9½-inch disc wheels. ½-inch rubber tires.

Packing—For easy assembly. Weight per crate, 50 lbs.

No. 1512 OVERLAND

Same as No. 1513 Overland described above, except packed
K. D., one in carton.   Weight per carton, 40 lbs.

No. 1507 DODGE

Length Overall—33 inches.

Finish—Jade green, trimmed with white and Paradise green. Paradise green wheels.

Equipment—As shown.

Gear—Adjustable rubber pedals.

Wheels—8-inch disc wheels. ⅝-inch rubber tires.

Packing—One in carton, K. D. Weight per carton, 27 lbs.

No. 1509 DᴇSOTO

Length Overall—35 inches.

Finish—Red, trimmed with white. Red wheels.

Equipment—As shown, including electric head lights.

Gear—Ball bearing. Adjustable rubber pedals.

Wheels—9½-inch disc wheels. ¾-inch rubber tires.

Packing—One in carton, K. D. Weight per carton, 34 lbs.

No. 1515 NASH

Length Overall—42 inches.

Finish—Buff, with tan trim and orange striping. Tan fenders. Buff wheels.

Equipment—As shown, including Pierce Arrow type electric head lights.

Gear—Ball bearing. Adjustable rubber pedals.

Wheels—9½-inch disc wheels. ⅝-inch rubber tires.

Packing—For easy assembly. Weight per crate, 52 lbs.

No. 1514 NASH

Same as No. 1515 Nash described above, except packed K. D., one in carton. Weight per carton, 42 lbs.

No. 1517 STUDEBAKER

Length Overall—44 inches.

Finish—Red, with cream trim and black striping. Cream fenders. Red wheels.

Equipment—As shown, including streamline fenders.

Gear—Adjustable rubber pedals.

Wheels—9½-inch disc wheels. ⅝-inch rubber tires.

Packing—For easy assembly. Weight per crate, 50 lbs.

No. 1516 STUDEBAKER

Same as No. 1517 Studebaker described above, except packed K. D., one in carton. Weight per carton, 40 lbs.

No. 1519 HUDSON

Length Overall—45 inches.

Finish—Cream, with green trim and black striping. Green fenders. Cream wheels.

Equipment—As shown, including Pierce Arrow type electric head lights, French horn and streamline fenders.

Gear—Ball bearing. Adjustable rubber pedals.

Wheels—9½-inch spoke type disc wheels. ¾-inch rubber tires.

Packing—For easy assembly. Weight per crate, 60 lbs.

No. 1518 HUDSON

Same as No. 1519 Hudson described above, except packed K. D., one in carton. Weight per carton, 50 lbs.

No. 1521 AUBURN

Length Overall—45 inches.

Finish—Tan, with green trim and white striping. Green fenders. Tan wheels.

Equipment—As shown, including Pierce Arrow type electric head lights, French horn and streamline fenders.

Gear—Ball bearing. Adjustable rubber pedals.

Wheels—10-inch disc wheels with high grade ball bearings. 2.50″ Firestone gum dipped balloon tires.

Packing—For easy assembly. Weight per crate, 70 lbs.

No. 1520 AUBURN

Same as No. 1521 Auburn described above, except packed K. D., one in carton. Weight per carton, 60 lbs.

No. 5607 S. U. AIRFLOW DeSOTO

Length Overall—46 inches.

Finish—Red, trimmed with cream. Fenders cream. Wheels red.

Equipment—As shown, including DeSoto type electric head lights.

Gear—Ball bearing. Adjustable rubber pedals.

Wheels—9½-inch disc wheels. ¾-inch rubber tires.

Packing—For easy assembly. Weight per crate, 65 lbs.

No. 5607 AIRFLOW DeSOTO

Same as No. 5607 S. U. described above, except packed K. D.,
one in carton. Weight per carton, 55 lbs.

No. 5611 AIRFLOW CHRYSLER

Length Overall—51 inches.

Finish—Brown, trimmed with cream and tan. Fenders tan. Wheels brown.

Equipment—As shown, including Chrysler type electric head lights.

Gear—Ball bearing. Adjustable rubber pedals.

Wheels—10-inch spoke type disc wheels. 1-inch rubber tires.

Packing—For easy assembly. Weight per crate, 70 lbs.

No. 1523 BUICK

Length Overall—45 inches.

Finish—Black, with cream trim and orange striping. Cream fenders and wheels.

Equipment—As shown, including Hupmobile type electric head lights, electric horn and streamline fenders.

Gear—Ball bearing. Adjustable rubber pedals.

Wheels—9½-inch spoke type disc wheels. ¾-inch rubber tires.

Packing—For easy assembly. Weight per crate, 62 lbs.

No. 1522 BUICK

Same as No. 1523 Buick described above, except packed K. D., one in carton. Weight per carton, 52 lbs.

No. 1525 LaSALLE

Length Overall—49 inches.

Finish—Two-tone green, with white striping. Light green fenders. Dark green wheels with white stripe.

Equipment—As shown, including Pierce Arrow type electric head lights, electric horn, streamline fenders, gear shift, instrument board, padded seat and new type cadmium plated bumper.

Gear—Ball bearing. Adjustable rubber pedals.

Wheels—10-inch spoke type disc wheels. 1-inch rubber tires.

Packing—For easy assembly. Weight per crate, 72 lbs.

No. 1528 GRAHAM

Length Overall—50 inches.

Finish—Tan, with cream trim and orange striping. Tan fenders. Cream wheels. Chromium plated louvers.

Equipment—As shown, including Hupmobile type electric head lights, electric horn, nickel plated adjustable windshield, gear shift, instrument board, cadmium plated steering wheel, new type cadmium plated bumper, padded seat and enclosed rear fenders.

Gear—Ball bearing. Adjustable rubber pedals.

Wheels—10-inch disc wheels with high grade ball bearings. 2.50" Firestone gum dipped balloon tires.

Packing—For easy assembly. Weight per crate, 72 lbs.

No. 1527 GRAHAM

Same as No. 1528 Graham described above, except equipped with 10-inch spoke type disc wheels. 1-inch rubber tires. Weight per crate, 72 lbs.

No. 1529 PACKARD

Length Overall—50 inches.

Finish—White, with green trim. Green fenders and wheels. Chromium plated deluxe bumper and louvers.

Equipment—As shown, including Pierce Arrow type electric head lights, French horn, nickel plated adjustable windshield with side wings and mirror, gear shift, instrument board, nickel plated steering wheel, padded seat and enclosed rear fenders.

Gear—Ball bearing. Adjustable rubber pedals.

Wheels—Auto spoke steel wheels. Roller bearing. 1½-inch rubber tires.

Packing—For easy assembly. Weight per crate, 76 lbs.

No. 1531 CORD

Length Overall—51 inches.

Finish—Red, with black trim and white striping. Red fenders and wheels. Chromium plated deluxe bumper and louvers.

Equipment—As shown, including Hupmobile type electric head lights and tail light. Electric horn, nickel plated adjustable windshield, gear shift, instrument board, nickel plated steering wheel, parking lights, rear metal hood, full upholstered seat and enclosed rear fenders.

Gear—Ball bearing. Adjustable rubber pedals. Rear springs.

Wheels—Auto spoke steel wheels. Roller bearing. 1½-inch rubber tires. Spare wheel and tire regularly furnished as shown.

Packing—For easy assembly. Weight per crate, 86 lbs.

No. 1534 CADILLAC

Length Overall—56 inches.

Finish—Black, with cream trim and orange striping. Cream fenders and wheels. Chromium plated lamps, bumper, radiator front and louvers.

Equipment—As shown, including bullet type electric head lights and tail light. Electric horn, nickel plated adjustable windshield with side wings and rear view mirror, gear shift, instrument board, nickel plated steering wheel, parking lights, rear metal hood, full upholstered seat and enclosed rear fenders.

Gear—Ball bearing. Adjustable rubber pedals. Rear springs.

Wheels—10-inch disc wheels equipped with 2.50″ Firestone gum dipped balloon tires. Ball bearing. Spare wheel and tire regularly furnished as shown.

Packing—For easy assembly. Weight per crate, 86 lbs.

No. 1533 CADILLAC

Same as No. 1534 Cadillac described above, except equipped with roller bearing auto spoke steel wheels with 1½-inch rubber tires. Weight per crate, 86 lbs.

No. 1551 FIRE CAPTAIN

Length Overall—30 inches.

Finish—Red, trimmed with white. Red wheels.

Equipment—As shown.

Gear—Adjustable rubber pedals.

Wheels—8-inch disc wheels. ½-inch rubber tires.

Packing—One in carton, K. D. Weight per carton, 22 lbs.

No. 1553 FIRE CAPTAIN

Length Overall—31 inches.

Finish—White enamel, trimmed with red and green. Red wheels.

Equipment—As shown.

Gear—Adjustable rubber pedals.

Wheels—8-inch disc wheels. ½-inch rubber tires.

Packing—One in carton, K. D. Weight per carton, 26 lbs.

No. 1556 FIRE CHIEF

Length Overall—36 inches.

Finish—White, trimmed with red and green. Red wheels.

Equipment—As shown, including electric head lights.

Gear—Ball bearing. Adjustable rubber pedals.

Wheels—9½-inch disc wheels. ¾-inch rubber tires.

Packing—One in carton, K. D. Weight per carton, 33 lbs.

No. 1555 FIRE CHIEF

Same as No. 1556 Fire Chief described above, except finished in red, with white trim, and with non-electric head lights. Weight per carton, 31 lbs.

No. 1559 FIRE CHIEF

Length Overall—40 inches.

Finish—Red, trimmed with white. Fenders and wheels red.

Equipment—As shown, including electric head lights.

Gear—Ball bearing. Adjustable rubber pedals.

Wheels—9½-inch disc wheels. ⅝-inch rubber tires.

Packing—For easy assembly. Weight per crate, 52 lbs.

No. 1558 FIRE CHIEF

Same as No. 1559 Fire Chief described above, except packed K. D., one in carton. Weight per carton, 42 lbs.

No. 444 REPUBLIC DUMP TRUCK

Size of Body	Wheels	Tires	Weight per Carton
16″ x 40″	10″	1″	49 lbs.

Specifications

Body—Frame and body made of hardwood shellaced and varnished.

Dump Box—As shown. Mechanical dumping mechanism which raises and lowers box and opens and closes end gate in same operation.

Siren—High speed siren, operates by pushing plunger, producing a shrill shriek.

Gong Bell—Regular equipment on foot rail as shown.

Gear—Channel steel reinforced with steel braces.

Wheels—Double disc. Self-retained roller bearings. Nickel plated hub caps.

Handle—Curved tubing with loop grip.

Finish—Silk green dump box, wheels, handle and foot rail. Body natural varnish finish with silk green stripe.

Packing—One in carton.

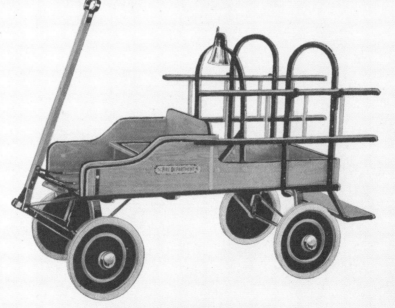

No. 448 FIRE TRUCK

Size of Body	Wheels	Tires	Weight per Carton
16″ x 36″	10″	1″	54 lbs.

Specifications

Body—Made of hardwood, reinforced with cleats.

Equipment—Tubing hand rails, rear step, two ladders, large bell.

Siren—High speed siren, operates by pushing plunger, producing a shrill shriek.

Gong Bell—Regular equipment on foot rail as shown.

Gear—Channel steel reinforced with steel braces.

Wheels—Double disc. Self-retained roller bearings. Nickel plated hub caps.

Finish—Natural varnish finish, trimmed with red. Red tubing uprights, wheels and foot rail.

Packing—One in carton.

NEW AMERICAN FEATURES

BALL BEARING STEERING GEAR

The above demonstrates our new front gear with ball bearing steering knuckles. Another of American's important mechanical improvements Regular equipment on all popular priced models.

HI-SPEED SIREN

Standard equipment on Fire Chief autos, Fire Apparatus, Police Scout Cars, and Fire Chief Velocipedes.

Illustration of steering wheel showing our modern control switch for electric headlights. Three positions—bright, dim, and off. Standard equipment on all popular priced juvenile autos.

AMERICAN'S Anti-Friction Gear

More Power
Greater Speed
Quicker Acceleration
and Less Effort with

HI-SPEED BALL BEARING PROPELLING GEAR

The outstanding mechanical refinement in juvenile automobiles—impressive in quality, design, and performance.

Friction in plain-bearing construction at vital points in the propelling mechanism of large juvenile automobiles has, in the past, restricted sales, impaired real pleasure, reduced power, and limited speed.

American-National engineers have overcome this handicap by designing the Hi-Speed Ball-Bearing Propelling Gear. This new ball bearing construction minimizes friction, eliminates lost motion at all essential points.

A moderate pressure on the pedals now gives immediate action with greater speed and more power.

No. 4567 WHITE TON TRUCK

This sturdy White Dump Truck is a favorite for kiddies from three to five years of age.

Length Overall—52½ inches.
Width Overall—19 inches.
Finish—Red and black, trimmed in yellow.
Dumping Box—13¾ x 18 inches heavy metal. End gate automatically opens and closes when box is raised or lowered. Finish black.

Gear—Ball bearing drive rods and steering gear. Adjustable rubber pedals.
Wheels—10-inch disc. **1-inch** rubber tires.
Equipment—Electric headlights (less batteries). **Rooter** horn. Balance as shown.
Packed—For easy set-up. Weight 61 lbs.

No. 4566 WHITE TON TRUCK

Same as above packed K. D. Weight 51 lbs.

No. 4568 WHITE HEAVY DUTY
(Dual Rear Wheels)

This realistic model out of the White Fleet will always be popular as it is built for heavy duty service and gives a youngster plenty of action.

Length Overall—55 inches.
Width Overall—21 inches.
Finish—Black and red, trimmed in yellow.
Gear—Full ball bearing drive rods and steering gear. Adjustable rubber pedals.

Dumping Box—15 x 17¾ inches heavy metal. End **gate** automatically opens and closes when box is raised **or** lowered. Finished red.

Wheels—Six 10-inch disc. **1-inch** rubber tires.

Equipment—Electric head and spot light (less batteries). Rooter horn. Fenders. Balance as shown.

Packed—For easy set-up. Weight 89 lbs.

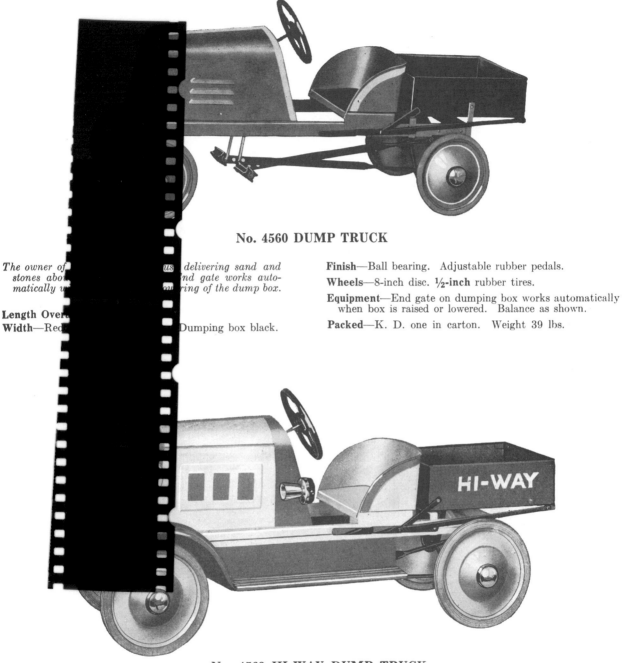

No. 4560 DUMP TRUCK

The owner of ⬛ *delivering sand and* *stones abou* ⬛ *nd gate works auto-* *matically u* ⬛ *ring of the dump box.*

Length Over

Width—Red ⬛ Dumping box black.

Finish—Ball bearing. Adjustable rubber pedals.

Wheels—8-inch disc. ½-inch rubber tires.

Equipment—End gate on dumping box works automatically when box is raised or lowered. Balance as shown.

Packed—K. D. one in carton. Weight 39 lbs.

No. 4563 HI-WAY DUMP TRUCK

The kiddies will not have to wait long for buddy to cart *away the dirt from the cave they are digging, as this dump* *truck is built for speed.*

Length Overall—49½ inches.

Finish—Green with cream panels and red trim. Dumping box finished in green.

Dumping Box—13 x 12½ inches. Heavy steel. End gate automatically opens and closes when box is raised or lowered.

Gear—Ball bearing drive rods and steering gear. Adjustable rubber pedals.

Wheels—10-inch disc. ¾-inch rubber tires.

Equipment—Electric headlights (less batteries). Rooter horn. Balance as shown.

Packed—For easy set-up. Weight 55 lbs.

No. 4562 DUMP TRUCK

Same as above except packed K. D. Weight 45 lbs.

Page 12

No. 4572 FIRE CHIEF

A Fire Chief for the little tots equipped with gong bell.

Length Overall—31 inches.

Finish—White enamel with red panels and striping.

Gear—Adjustable rubber pedals.

Wheels—8-inch disc, ½-inch rubber tires.

Equipment—Fire bell. V type front. Balance as shown.

Packed—One in carton, K. D. Weight 26 pounds.

No. 4574 FIRE CHIEF

This easy running model equipped with Fire Chief siren and gong bell provides a real thrill in playing fire.

Length Overall—35 inches.

Finish—Fire red with white panels and white striping.

Gear—**Ball bearing drive rods and steering gear.** Adjustable rubber pedals.

Wheels—10-inch disc. ¾-inch rubber tires.

Equipment—Electric head lights (less batteries). Nickel plated bell. Fire siren. Balance as shown.

Packed—One in carton, K. D. Weight 35 pounds.

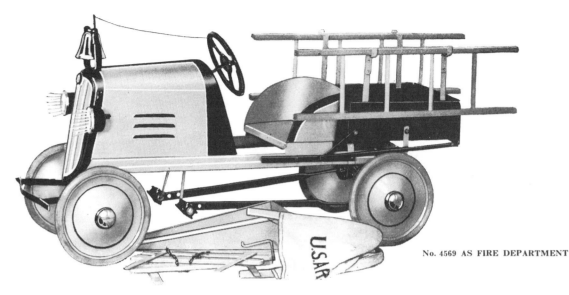

No. 4569 AS FIRE DEPARTMENT

No. 4569 FIVE-IN-ONE COMBINATION

Every child likes to build his own. This five-in-one combination enables him to have a dump truck, wrecking car, stake body truck, fire truck and army truck all in one.

Length Overall—48½ inches (Ladders not extending).
Finish—Red with black trim and white striping.

Gear—**Ball bearing.** Adjustable rubber pedals.
Wheels—10-inch disc. **⅝-inch** rubber tires.
Equipment—As shown in the various cuts on this page.
Packed—K. D. one in carton. Weight 47 lbs.

Convertible Changes Easily Made by Child

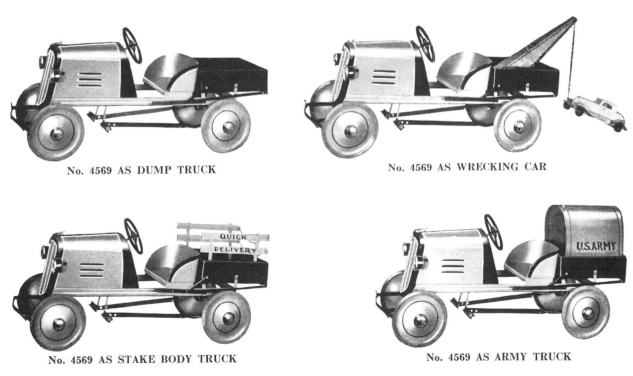

No. 4569 AS DUMP TRUCK

No. 4569 AS WRECKING CAR

No. 4569 AS STAKE BODY TRUCK

No. 4569 AS ARMY TRUCK

Page 14

No. 4576 FIRE CHIEF

A new Fire Chief which is an instant seller for parents know it will keep the youngsters interested the year around.

Length Overall—42 inches.

Finish—White with fire red panels and striping.

Gear—Ball bearing drive rods and steering gear. Adjustable rubber pedals.

Wheels—10-inch spoke type disc wheels. ¾-inch rubber tires.

Equipment—Bullet type electric headlights (less batteries). Nickeled bell. Fire siren. Modern streamline fenders. Front fender apron. Balance as shown.

Packed—For easy set-up. Weight 55 pounds.

No. 4575 FIRE CHIEF

Same as above except packed K. D. Weight 45 pounds.

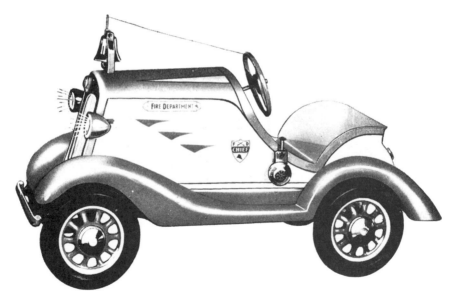

No. 4579 FIRE CHIEF

Every boy will rush to ask Dad for this big attractive Fire Chief equipped with new AUTOSPOKE wheels which will make all the children in the neighborhood envious.

Length Overall—43 inches.

Finish—White enamel with red panels and green striping.

Gear—Full ball bearing drive rods and steering gear. Adjustable rubber pedals. Rear springs.

Wheels—New AUTOSPOKE type. Roller bearing. 10-inch diameter, 1½-inch rubber tires.

Equipment—Bullet type electric headlights (less batteries). Nickeled fire bell. Fire siren. Modern streamline fenders. Front fender apron. Instrument board. Balance as shown.

Packed—For easy set-up. Weight 65 pounds.

No. 4578 FIRE CHIEF

Same as No. 4579 except packed K. D. Weight 55 pounds.

No. 4581 SCOUT CAR

Youngsters love to play cop and they'll flock around this ball bearing Scout Car the minute they see it.

Length Overall—42 inches.

Finish—Bright red with cream panels and black striping.

Gear—**Ball bearing drive rods and steering gear** rear springs, adjustable rubber pedals.

Wheels—10-inch spoke type disc. ¾-**inch** tires.

Equipment—Bullet type electric head lights (less batteries). Police siren. Pedestal bell. Modern streamline fenders. Front fender apron. Balance as shown.

Packed—For easy set-up. Weight 61 pounds.

No. 4580 SCOUT CAR

Same as No. 4581 except packed K. D. Weight 51 pounds.

No. 4577 FIRE PATROL

The kiddies will never tire of this Fire Patrol which permits a ladder man to ride on the rear. Full ball bearing gear assures easy running.

Length Overall—49 inches.

Finish—Fire red trimmed in yellow.

Gear—**Full ball bearing drive rods and steering gear.** Adjustable rubber pedals.

Wheels—10-inch spoke type disc. **1-inch** rubber tires.

Equipment—Bullet type electric head lights (less batteries). Fire siren. Instrument board. Two ladders. Rear platform. Balance as shown.

Packed—K. D. one in carton. Weight 51 pounds.

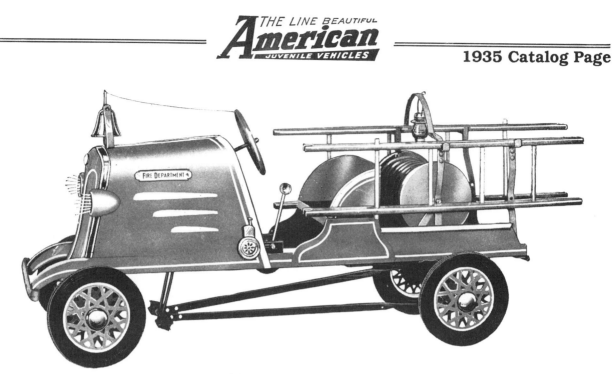

No. 4582 HOSE AUTO

This ball bearing model won't stay on the floor long after sonny's dad gets the alarm.

Length Overall—54-inches (Ladders extending)

Finish—Fire red trimmed in yellow.

Gear—Ball bearing drive rods and steering gear. Adjustable rubber pedals.

Wheels—10-inch spoke type disc. ¾-inch rubber tires.

Equipment—Bullet type electric headlights (less batteries). Fire siren. Gear shift. Balance as shown.

Packed—One in crate K. D. Weight 90 pounds.

No. 4583 HOSE AUTO

A new and fully equipped Hose Cart with real play value for the active youngsters.

Length Overall—56-inches.

Finish—Fire red trimmed in yellow.

Gear—Full ball bearing drive rods and steering gear. Adjustable rubber pedals.

Wheels—10-inch spoke type disc. 1-inch rubber tires.

Equipment—Electric headlights (less batteries). Fire siren. Balance as shown.

Packed—For easy set-up. Weight 100 pounds.

Page 18

70

No. 4584 HOSE AUTO

This is a two-passenger model strong enough for an extra fireman to hang on the rear. This feature, coupled with Headlights, Hose and Signal Lights, makes it one of the very best sellers.

Length Overall—65 inches (Ladders extending).

Finish—Fire red. Trimmed in yellow.

Gear—**Full ball bearing drive rods and steering gear.** Adjustable rubber pedals.

Wheels—12-inch Rolls auto wheels. Roller bearing. **1-inch** rubber tires.

Equipment—Electric head lights and spot light (less batteries). Hose with nozzle. Fire siren. Rear signal lights with elaborate nickel trim. Chromium plated steering wheel. Instrument board.

Packed—For easy set-up. Weight 132 lbs.

No. 4586 FIRE TOWER

Unusually complete equipment draws the kiddies to this model in droves. A whole gang will play with it day after day.

Length Overall—70 inches (Tower extending).

Finish—Fire red. Trimmed in yellow.

Gear—**Full ball bearing drive rods and steering gear.** Adjustable rubber pedals.

Wheels—12-inch Rolls auto wheels. Roller bearing. **1-inch** rubber tires.

Equipment—Electric head and spot light (less batteries). Fire siren. Instrument board. Gear shift. Upholstered seat. Chromium plated steering wheel.

Packed—For easy set-up. Weight 135 lbs.

Page 19

No. 4592 WASP

Kiddies are air-minded and this Wasp plane will afford them many hours of amusement.

Length Overall—40 inches. Wing spread 24 inches.
Finish—Bolera cream. Trimmed in red and green.

Wheels—Front 8 x ⅝-inch rubber tires; rear, 6 x ½-inch rubber tired disc.
Equipment—Revolving propeller. Balance as shown.
Packed—One in carton, K. D. Weight 31 lbs.

The propeller revolves when the plane is in motion making Sonny feel like a real Air pilot.

No. 4594 AIR PILOT

Length Overall—51 inches. Wing spread 30 inches.
Finish—Tangerine. Trimmed in sea green and yellow.
Wheels—Front, 10 x ⅝-inch rubber tires; rear, 7 x ½-inch rubber tired disc.
Equipment—Propeller revolves as plane is in motion.

Packed—One in carton, K. D. Weight 41 lbs.

No. 4595 AIR PILOT

Same as No. 4594 above except furnished with 10 x ¾-inch balloon disc wheels. Finish—Body black. Wings red. Striping, cream. Weight 42 lbs.

No. 4506 OVERLAND

A lightweight closed body roadster for children two to three years of age.

Length Overall—31-inches.

Finish—American red with yellow trim.

Gear—Adjustable rubber pedals.

Wheels—8-inch disc. ½-**inch** rubber tires.

Equipment—V-type radiator front. Balance as shown.

Packed—One in carton, K. D. Weight, 25 lbs.

No. 4507 CHEVROLET

A sporty car for the little tots. Equipped with real electric lights.

Length Overall—32 inches.

Finish—Jade green with tan panels and black striping.

Gear—Adjustable rubber pedals.

Wheels—8-inch disc. ½-**inch** rubber tires.

Equipment—Electric headlights (less batteries). V type radiator front. Balance as shown.

Packed—One in carton, K. D. Weight 27 lbs.

No. 4508 DODGE

A real thrill strikes the kiddies who see this car equipped with electric headlights, ball bearing gear and windshield.

Length Overall—34 inches.

Finish—Cream with red panels and green striping.

Gear—**Ball bearing.** Adjustable rubber pedals.

Wheels—8½-inch disc. ⅝-**inch** rubber tires.

Equipment—Electric headlights (less batteries). V type radiator front. Balance as shown.

Packed—One in carton, K. D. Weight 28 lbs.

Page 3

No. 4510 ESSEX

A new model for three-year olds with fenders, windshield, electric head lights and ball bearing gear. Has a strong sales appeal to parents.

Length Overall—38 inches.

Finish—Tangerine with black panels and white striping.

Gear—**Ball bearing.** Adjustable rubber pedals.

Wheels—9½-inch disc. ⅝-inch rubber tires.

Equipment—Electric head lights (less batteries). V type radiator front. Balance as shown.

Packed—One in carton, K. D. Weight 38 pounds.

No. 4511 Essex

Same as No. 4510 except packed for easy set up. Weight 48 pounds.

No. 4512 ACE

This open side racing model with ball bearing gear fairly urges the kiddies to get in and break the speed limit.

Length Overall—35 inches.

Finish—Paradise green with cream panels and orange striping.

Gear— **Ball bearing drive rods and steering gear.** Adjustable rubber pedals.

Wheels—9½-inch disc. ⅝-inch rubber tires.

Equipment—Electric head lights (less batteries). V type radiator front. Balance as shown.

Packed—One in carton, K. D. Weight 34 lbs.

No. 4514 REO

A snappy roadster. Electric headlights, windshield and rooter horn are regular equipment on this popular seller.

Length Overall—35 inches.

Finish—Red with black panels and white striping.

Gear—**Ball bearing drive rods and steering gear.** Adjustable rubber pedals.

Wheels—10-inch disc. ¾-inch rubber tires.

Equipment—Electric head lights (less batteries). V type radiator front. Balance as shown.

Packed—One in carton, K. D. Weight 36 pounds.

No. 4516 MASTER SIX

The kiddies instantly flock to this model equipped with realistic rear trunk for carrying tools. Real electric headlights add to its appeal.

Length Overall—38 inches.

Finish—Cream with tan panels and black striping.

Gear—**Ball bearing drive rods and steering gear.** Adjustable rubber pedals.

Wheels—10-inch spoke type disc. 1-inch rubber tires.

Equipment—Bullet type electric head lights (less batteries). V type radiator front. Balance as shown.

Packed—One in carton, K. D. Weight 40 pounds.

Page 5

No. 4519 PONTIAC

This new model with streamline fenders and bullet type electric headlights promises the youngster many hours of enjoyment.

Length Overall—40½ inches.

Finish—Jade green with Forest green panels and yellow striping.

Gear—Ball bearing drive rods and steering gear. Adjustable rubber pedals.

Wheels—10-inch disc. ¾-**inch** rubber tires.

Equipment—Bullet type electric headlights (less batteries) Modern streamline fenders. Front fender apron. Balance as shown.

Packed—For easy set-up. Weight 50 pounds.

No. 4518 PONTIAC

Same as No. 4519 except packed K. D. Weight 40 lbs.

No. 4521 BUICK

Every youngster will be keen for this 1934 model equipped with new spoke type wheels.

Length Overall—42 inches.

Finish—Red with black panels and white striping.

Gear—Ball bearing drive rods and steering gear. Adjustable rubber pedals.

Wheels—10-inch spoke type disc. ¾-**inch** rubber tires.

Equipment—Bullet type electric headlights (less batteries). Modern streamline fenders. Front fender apron. Balance as shown.

Packed—For easy set-up. Weight 55 pounds.

No. 4520 BUICK

Same as No. 4521 except packed K. D. Weight 45 pounds.

No. 4523 NASH

A new streamline roadster for the modern minded kiddies.

Length Overall—47 inches.
Finish—Paradise green with orange panels and white striping.
Gear—**Ball bearing drive rods and steering gear.** Adjustable rubber pedals.
Wheels—10-inch disc. ¾-**inch** rubber tires.

Equipment—Bullet type electric headlights (less batteries). Modern streamline fenders. Front fender apron. Instrument board. Balance as shown.

Packed—For easy set-up. Weight 60 pounds.

No. 4522 NASH

Same as No. 4523 except packed K. D. Weight 50 pounds.

No. 4525 STUDEBAKER

One of our most popular sellers. It has ball bearings in pedal hangers and rear axle. Its speed and easy riding qualities appeal to children from four to six years of age.

Length Overall—45 inches.
Finish—Black with orange panels and white striping.
Gear—**Full ball bearing drive rods and steering gear.** Adjustable rubber pedals.

Wheels—10-inch spoke type disc. ¾-**inch** rubber tires.

Equipment—Bullet type electric headlights (less batteries). Instrument board. Front fender apron. New type streamline bumper. Balance as shown.

Packed—For easy set-up. Weight 61 lbs.

No. 4524 STUDEBAKER

Same as No. 4525 except packed K. D. Weight 51 pounds.

No. 4526 HUPMOBILE

Just like Dad's, with spare wheel, padded seat, electric lights and full ball bearing gear.

Length Overall—45 inches.

Finish—Bolera cream with Russell brown panels and black striping.

Gear—**Full ball bearing drive rods and steering gear.** Rear springs. Adjustable rubber pedals.

Wheels—10-inch spoke type disc. **1-inch** rubber tires.

Equipment—Bullet type electric head lights (less batteries). Modern streamline fenders. Front fender apron. Gear shift. Three-piece windshield. Padded seat. Instrument board. New style streamline bumper. Balance as shown.

Packed—For easy set-up. Weight 72 lbs.

No. 4530 PACKARD

Keep plenty of this number in stock. A fast selling model with 1934 stream line fenders, rear vision mirror, padded seat, V type radiator front, and all features which appeal to children from four and one-half to seven years of age.

Length Overall—49 inches.

Finish—Blue-green with yellow panels and red striping.

Gear—**Full ball bearing drive rods and steering gear.** Rear springs. Adjustable rubber pedals.

Wheels—10-inch spoke type disc. **1-inch** rubber tires.

Equipment—Bullet type electric head lights (less batteries). Modern streamline fenders. Gear shift. Front fender apron. Padded seat. Instrument board. Rear vision mirror. New style streamline bumper. Balance as shown.

Packed—For easy set-up. Weight 73 lbs.

No. 4532 LaSALLE

This new model finished in white with lavender trim and equipped with 1934 style Autospoke wheels will be the talk of the neighborhood.

Length Overall—49 inches.

Finish—Porcelain white enamel with lavender panels and green striping.

Gear—**Full ball bearing drive rods and steering gear.** Rear springs. Adjustable rubber pedals.

Wheels—New AUTOSPOKE type. Roller bearing. 10-inch diameter, 1½-inch rubber tires.

Equipment—Bullet type electric head lights and tail light (less batteries). Modern streamline fenders. Front fender apron. Gear shift. Instrument board. Padded seat. Chromium plated windshield and lamps. New style streamline bumper. Balance as shown.

Packed—For easy set-up. Weight 76 lbs.

No. 4534 CADILLAC

The kiddies will flock to this spare wheel job which is just like Dad's car, electric lights and everything.

Length Overall—49 inches.

Finish—Two-tone green with yellow striping.

Gear—**Full ball bearing drive rods and steering gear.** Rear springs. Adjustable rubber pedals.

Wheels—New AUTOSPOKE type. Roller bearing. 10-inch diameter, 1½-inch rubber tires.

Equipment—Bullet type electric headlights and tail light (less batteries). Modern streamline fenders. Front fender apron. Gear shift. Instrument board. Padded seat. License tag. Chromium plated radiator front, lamps, windshield and steering wheel. New style streamline bumper. Balance as shown.

Packed—For easy set-up. Weight 80 lbs.

No. 4546 TANDEM

It is only natural for children to get lonesome, and this Tandem auto enables them to take a ride together. Action for both of them, as it is equipped with tandem pedal drive.

Length Overall—66-inches.

Finish—American red with black panel and yellow striping.

Gear—**Full ball bearing drive rods and steering gear.** Adjustable rubber pedals.

Wheels—12-inch Rolls auto wheels. Roller bearing, **1-inch** rubber tires.

Equipment—Electric head lights (less batteries). Upholstered seat. Instrument board. Chromium plated steering wheel and bumper. Balance as shown.

Packed—For easy set-up. Weight 111 pounds.

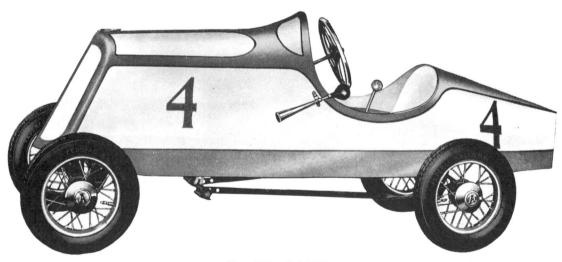

No. 4554 RACER

Whenever the sun shines you will find buddy searching for a speedway with this fast 1934 racing model.

Length Overall—67-inches.

Finish—White enamel with heavy red panels and green striping.

Gear—**Full ball bearing drive rods and steering gear.** Adjustable rubber pedals.

Wheels—Ball bearing, nickel plated spokes, chromium plated hub caps. Tires 2.50x12.75 balloon pneumatics, heavy non-skid tread.

Equipment—Instrument board. Balance as shown.

Packed—For easy set-up. Weight 86 pounds.

No. 4552 RACER

Same as No. 4554 with 12-inch Rolls auto wheels. Roller bearing. **1-inch** rubber tires.

Page 11

No. 4536 LOCOMOBILE

A child certainly will write Santa Claus when he sees this 1934 snappy model with all modern equipment on your floor.

Length Overall—52 inches.

Finish—American red with black panels and white striping.

Gear—**Full ball bearing drive rods and steering gear.** Adjustable rubber pedals. Rear springs.

Wheels—New AUTOSPOKE type. Roller bearing. 10-inch diameter, **1½-inch** rubber tires.

Equipment—Bullet type electric head lights and tail light (less batteries). Modern streamline fenders. Front fender apron. Gear shift. Chromium plated windshield, steering wheel, radiator front and lamps. New style streamline bumper. Full upholstered seat. Instrument board. Gear shift. License tag. Balance as shown.

Packed—For easy set-up. Weight 86 pounds.

NO. 4538 LINCOLN

A beautiful and completely equipped roadster which parents of children five to eight years old find difficulty in resisting.

Length Overall—56 inches.

Finish—Black with cream panels and orange striping.

Gear—**Full ball bearing drive rods and steering gear.** Rear springs. Adjustable rubber pedals.

Wheels—New AUTOSPOKE type. Roller bearing. 10-inch diameter, **1½-inch** rubber tires.

Equipment—Bullet type electric head lights and tail light (less batteries). Modern streamline fenders. Front fender apron. Full upholstered seat. Instrument board. Chromium plated radiator front, lamps, windshield and steering wheel. Gear shift. New style streamline bumper. Balance as shown.

Packed—For easy set-up. Weight 86 pounds.

No. 1681 GARFORD TRUCK

Length Overall—45 inches.

Finish—Red, trimmed with white. Wheels red with white stripe. Dump box red.

Equipment—As shown. Dump box operated by handle beside driver's seat.

Gear—Adjustable rubber pedals.

Wheels—10-inch disc wheels. ½-inch rubber tires.

Packing—One in carton, K. D. Weight per carton, 39 lbs.

No. 1683 REPUBLIC TRUCK

Length Overall—47 inches.

Finish—Green, trimmed with cream. Wheels green with cream stripe. Dump box green.

Equipment—As shown. Dump box operated by handle beside driver's seat.

Gear—Adjustable rubber pedals.

Wheels—9½-inch disc wheels. ⅝-inch rubber tires.

Packing—One in carton, K. D. Weight per carton, 55 lbs.

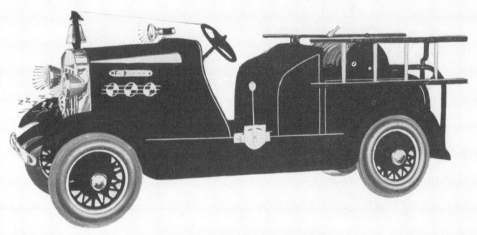

No. 1673 HOSE CART

Length Overall—57 inches (ladders extending).

Finish—White, trimmed with red. Wheels red with white stripe. Fenders red.

Equipment—As shown, including electric head lights and spot light, less batteries. Nickel plated fire bell, Fire Chief siren, gear shift lever, Blue Streak motor hummer and two ladders. Real rubber hose with brass nozzle and hydrant attachment.

Gear—Ball bearing. Adjustable rubber pedals.

Wheels—10-inch spoke type disc wheels. 1-inch rubber tires.

Packing—One in carton, K. D. Weight per carton, 88 lbs.

No. 1675 HOSE CART

Length Overall—64 inches (ladders extending).

Finish—Red, trimmed with white. Wheels red with white stripe. Fenders red.

Equipment—As shown, including electric head lights, horn and spot light, less batteries. Instrument board, gear shift lever and Blue Streak motor hummer. Real rubber hose with brass nozzle and hydrant attachment.

Gear—Ball bearing. Adjustable rubber pedals.

Wheels—12-inch Rolls auto wheels. Roller bearing. 1-inch rubber tires.

Packing—For easy assembly. Weight per crate, 120 lbs.

Children's Vehicles Since 1887

No. 1669 RADIO CRUISER

Length Overall—50 inches.

Finish—White, trimmed with red and green. Wheels green with white stripe. Fenders green.

Equipment—As shown, including electric head lights, less batteries, instrument board and Blue Streak motor hummer.

Gear—Ball bearing. Adjustable rubber pedals.

Wheels—10-inch auto spoke steel wheels. Roller bearing. 1½-inch rubber tires.

Packing—For easy assembly. Weight per crate, 70 lbs.

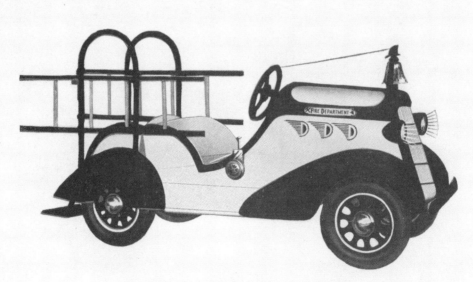

No. 1671 HOOK AND LADDER

Length Overall—52 inches.

Finish—White, trimmed with green and red. Wheels red with white stripe. Fenders red.

Equipment—As shown, including electric head lights, less batteries, and instrument board.

Gear—Ball bearing. Adjustable rubber pedals.

Wheels—10-inch auto spoke steel wheels. Roller bearing. 1½-inch rubber tires.

Packing—For easy assembly. Weight per crate, 73 lbs.

Children's Vehicles Since 1887

No. 1665 HOOK AND LADDER

Length Overall—41 inches.

Finish—Red, trimmed with white. Wheels red with white stripe. Aluminum front.

Equipment—As shown.

Gear—Adjustable rubber pedals.

Wheels—9½-inch disc wheels. ⅝-inch rubber tires.

Packing—One in carton, K. D. Weight per carton, 50 lbs.

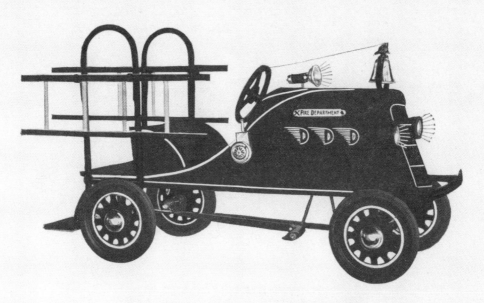

No. 1667 HOOK AND LADDER

Length Overall—49 inches.

Finish—Red, trimmed with white. Wheels red with white stripe.

Equipment—As shown, including electric head lights and spot light, less batteries.

Gear—Ball bearing. Adjustable rubber pedals.

Wheels—9½-inch spoke type disc wheels. ¾-inch rubber tires.

Packing—One in carton, K. D. Weight per carton, 55 lbs.

No. 1657 FIRE CAPTAIN
(Patent No. D-99,004)

Length Overall—41 inches.

Finish—Red, trimmed with white. Wheels red with white stripe. Aluminum front.

Equipment—As shown.

Gear—Adjustable rubber pedals.

Wheels—9½-inch disc wheels. ½-inch rubber tires.

Packing—One in carton, K. D. Weight per carton, 42 lbs.

No. 1659 FIRE CAPTAIN

Length Overall—44 inches.

Finish—White, trimmed with green and red. Wheels white with red stripe. Fenders red.

Equipment—As shown, including electric head lights, less batteries.

Gear—Adjustable rubber pedals.

Wheels—9½-inch disc wheels. ⅝-inch rubber tires.

Packing—One in carton, K. D. Weight per carton, 50 lbs.

(These Fire Captain autos covered by Trade Mark No. 317,054)

Children's Vehicles Since 1887

No. 1651 FIRE CAPTAIN

Length Overall—31 inches.

Finish—Red, trimmed with white. Wheels red with white stripe.

Equipment—As shown.

Gear—Adjustable rubber pedals.

Wheels—8-inch disc wheels. ½-inch rubber tires.

Packing—One in carton, K. D. Weight per carton, 28 lbs.

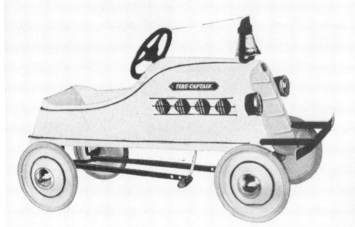

No. 1653 FIRE CAPTAIN

(Patent No. D-99,004)

Length Overall—35 inches.

Finish—White enamel, trimmed with red. Wheels white with red stripe.

Equipment—As shown.

Gear—Adjustable rubber pedals.

Wheels—8-inch disc wheels. ½-inch rubber tires.

Packing—One in carton, K. D. Weight per carton, 28 lbs.

No. 1655 FIRE CAPTAIN

Length Overall—35 inches.

Finish—Red, trimmed with white. Wheels red with white stripe.

Equipment—As shown.

Gear—Adjustable rubber pedals.

Wheels—9½-inch disc wheels. ⅝-inch rubber tires.

Packing—One in carton, K. D. Weight per carton, 34 lbs.

(These Fire Captain autos covered by Trade Mark No. 317,054)

No. 6619 SKIPPY RACER

Length Overall—44 inches.

Finish—White, trimmed with red. Wheels red.

Equipment—As shown, including instrument board and Blue Streak motor hummer.

Gear—Ball bearing. Adjustable rubber pedals.

Wheels—10-inch disc wheels equipped with two-inch pneumatic tires. Ball bearing.

Packing—For easy assembly. Weight per crate, 70 lbs.

No. 1661 G-MAN CRUISER

Length Overall—44 inches.

Finish—White, trimmed with green and red. Wheels white with green stripe. Fenders green.

Equipment—As shown, including realistic G-Man gun manufactured by Louis Marx & Company.

Gear—Adjustable rubber pedals.

Wheels—9½-inch disc wheels. ⅝-inch rubber tires.

Packing—One in carton, K. D. Weight per carton, 47 lbs.

Children's Vehicles Since 1887

No. 1625 CADILLAC

Length Overall—48 inches.

Finish—Dark blue, trimmed with cream and red. Wheels and fenders cream.

Equipment—As shown, including electric head lights and horn, less batteries. Sport type fenders, adjustable nickel plated windshield, nickel plated bumper, Blue Streak motor hummer, instrument board, padded seat and gear shift lever.

Gear—Ball bearing. Adjustable rubber pedals.

Wheels—10-inch spoke type disc wheels. 1-inch rubber tires.

Packing—For easy assembly. Weight per crate, 72 lbs.

No. 1627 LINCOLN

Length Overall—51 inches.

Finish—Red, trimmed with black and white. Wheels and fenders red.

Equipment—As shown, including electric head lights and horn, less batteries. Blue Streak motor hummer. Gear shift lever and instrument board. Upholstered seat and back.

Gear—Ball bearing. Adjustable rubber pedals.

Wheels—10-inch disc wheels equipped with two-inch pneumatic tires. Ball bearing.

Packing—For easy assembly. Weight per crate, 80 lbs.

No. 1626 LINCOLN

Same as No. 1627 Lincoln described above, except equipped with 10-inch spoke type disc wheels. 1-inch rubber tires.

Weight per crate, 76 lbs.

Children's Vehicles Since 1887

No. 1619 PACKARD

Length Overall—46 inches.

Finish—Maroon, trimmed with cream and red. Wheels and fenders red.

Equipment—As shown, including electric head lights and horn, less batteries. Sport type fenders and Blue Streak motor hummer.

Gear—Ball bearing. Adjustable rubber pedals.

Wheels—10-inch disc wheels equipped with two-inch pneumatic tires. Ball bearing.

Packing—For easy assembly. Weight per crate, 70 lbs.

No. 1618 PACKARD

Same as No. 1619 Packard described above, except equipped with 10-inch spoke type disc wheels. ¾-inch rubber tires.

Weight per crate, 66 lbs.

No. 1623 GRAHAM

Length Overall—47 inches.

Finish—Cream, trimmed with red and green. Wheels cream with red stripe. Fenders red.

Equipment—As shown, including bullet type electric head lights and horn, less batteries. Sport type fenders, Blue Streak motor hummer, padded seat, gear shift lever, nickel plated adjustable windshield, instrument board and nickel plated bumper.

Gear—Ball bearing. Adjustable rubber pedals.

Wheels—10-inch spoke type disc wheels. 1-inch rubber tires.

Packing—For easy assembly. Weight per crate, 62 lbs.

Children's Vehicles Since 1887

SKIPPY AUTOMOBILES

No. 6604 PONTIAC

Length Overall—44 inches.

Finish—Paradise green trimmed with white and black. Wheels green with white stripe. Fenders Paradise green.

Equipment—As shown.

Gear—Adjustable rubber pedals.

Wheels—9½-inch disc wheels. ⅝-inch rubber tires.

Packing—One in carton, K. D. Weight per carton, 45 lbs

No. 6605 CHRYSLER AIRFLOW

Length Overall—44 inches.

Finish—Red, trimmed with cream. Wheels cream with red stripe. Fenders red.

Equipment—As shown, including electric head lights, less batteries.

Gear—Ball bearing. Adjustable rubber pedals.

Wheels—9½-inch disc wheels. ⅝-inch rubber tires.

Packing—For easy assembly. Weight per carton, 55 lbs.

Special Note: The fenders on the No. 6605 Chrysler are permanently welded to the steel body, reducing setting up operations and costs to a minimum.

SEE SKIPPY RACER CATALOG FOR OTHER SKIPPY AUTOS

Children's Vehicles Since 1887

No. 1613 LaSALLE

Length Overall—43 inches.

Finish—Red, trimmed with cream. Wheels red with cream stripe. Fenders cream.

Equipment—As shown, including sport type fenders.

Gear—Adjustable rubber pedals.

Wheels—9½-inch disc wheels. ⅝-inch rubber tires.

Packing—One in carton, K. D. Weight per carton, 42 lbs.

No. 1617 BUICK

Length Overall—45 inches.

Finish—Light blue, trimmed with white and orange. Wheels white with orange stripe. Fenders blue.

Equipment—As shown, including electric head lights and horn, less batteries. Sport type fenders.

Gear—Ball bearing. Adjustable rubber pedals.

Wheels—9½-inch spoke type disc wheels. ¾-inch rubber tires.

Packing—One in carton, K. D. Weight per carton, 40 lbs.

Children's Vehicles Since 1887

No. 1607 NASH

Length Overall—37 inches.

Finish—Green, trimmed with cream. Wheels green with black center and cream stripe.

Equipment—As shown.

Gear—Adjustable rubber pedals.

Wheels—9½-inch disc wheels. ¾-inch rubber tires.

Packing—One in carton, K. D. Weight per carton, 34 lbs.

No. 1609 STUDEBAKER
(Patent No. D-99,004)

Length Overall—37 inches.

Finish—Red, trimmed with white. Wheels red with white stripe. Aluminum front.

Equipment—As shown, including electric head lights, less batteries.

Gear—Adjustable rubber pedals.

Wheels—9½-inch spoke type disc wheels. ¾-inch rubber tires.

Packing—One in carton, K. D. Weight per carton, 38 lbs.

No. 1611 HUDSON
(Patent No. D-99,004)

Length Overall—42 inches.

Finish—Buff, trimmed with green. Wheels green with buff stripe. Fenders green.

Equipment—As shown.

Gear—Adjustable rubber pedals.

Wheels—9½-inch spoke type disc wheels. ⅝-inch rubber tires.

Packing—One in carton, K. D. Weight per carton, 38 lbs.

Children's Vehicles Since 1887

No. 1601 CHEVROLET

Length Overall—33 inches.

Finish—Red, trimmed with white. Wheels red with white stripe.

Equipment—As shown.

Gear—Adjustable rubber pedals.

Wheels—8-inch disc wheels. ½-inch rubber tires.

Packing—One in carton, K. D. Weight per carton, 25 lbs.

No. 1603 DODGE

(Patent No. D-99,004)

Length Overall—36 inches.

Finish—Light blue, trimmed with white. Wheels blue with white stripe.

Equipment—As shown.

Gear—Adjustable rubber pedals.

Wheels—8-inch disc wheels. ½-inch rubber tires.

Packing—One in carton, K. D. Weight per carton, 27 lbs.

No. 1605 HUPMOBILE

(Patent No. D-99,004)

Length Overall—36 inches.

Finish—Red, trimmed with white. Wheels red with white stripe. Aluminum front.

Equipment—As shown, including electric head lights, less batteries.

Gear—Adjustable rubber pedals.

Wheels—8-inch disc wheels. ⅝-inch rubber tires.

Packing—One in carton, K. D. Weight per carton, 28 lbs.

No. 1604 HUPMOBILE

Same as No. 1605 Hupmobile described above, except equipped with non-electric head lights.

Children's Vehicles Since 1887

No. 1685 FORD V-8 TRUCK

Length Overall—49 inches.

Finish—French gray, trimmed with cream. Wheels cream with gray stripe. Fenders gray. Dump box, apron and running board cream.

Equipment—As shown, including electric head lights and spot light on cowl, less batteries. Dump box operated by handle beside driver's seat.

Gear—Ball bearing. Adjustable rubber pedals.

Wheels—10-inch disc wheels. 1-inch rubber tires.

Packing—One in carton, K. D. Weight per carton, 53 lbs.

No. 1687 WHITE TRUCK

Length Overall—55 inches.

Finish—White, trimmed with red and green. Wheels green with white stripe. Fenders, cowl and dump box green.

Equipment—As shown, including electric head lights, spot light on cowl and electric horn, less batteries. Dump box operated by handle beside driver's seat.

Gear—Ball bearing. Adjustable rubber pedals.

Wheels—10-inch disc wheels. 1-inch rubber tires.

Packing—One in carton, K. D. Weight per carton, 63 lbs.

Children's Vehicles Since 1887

No. 28-179

No. 28-133

No. 28-179—HOSE CART

BODY—Length overall 56-inches. Width at pedals 12-inches.

FINISH—Body, hood and seat red, striped and decorated in white. Wheels red, striped in white.

EQUIPMENT—As shown, including ball bearing high speed gear (ratio 2 to 1). Gears revolving in lubricant in sealed housing unit. Electric head lights. Electric spotlight. Rubber hose with nozzle and hydrant attachment. Siren.

WHEELS—10 x 1½-inch moulded rubber tire, artillery type.

WEIGHT—90 lbs. Packed set up for easy assembly, one in a crate.

No. 28-133—SKIPPY RACER

BODY—Length overall 55-inches. Width at pedals 12-inches.

FINISH—Body, hood and seat green, striped and decorated in white and yellow. Wheels white.

EQUIPMENT—As shown, including ball bearing high speed gear (ratio 2 to 1). Gears revolving in lubricant in sealed housing unit. Electric horn.

WHEELS—10 x 2¾-inch pneumatic tire, ball bearing disc.

WEIGHT—70 lbs. Packed set up for easy assembly, one in a crate.

No. 28-131

Same as No. 28-133, except 10 x 1-inch rubber tire artillery type wheels.

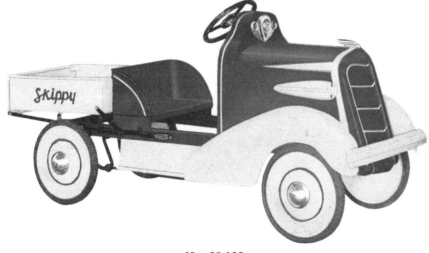

No. 28-195

No. 28-197

No. 28-195—DUMP TRUCK

BODY—Length overall 52-inches. Width at pedals 12-inches.

FINISH—Body, hood and seat blue, striped in cream. Dump box cream enameled. Fenders cream. Apron cream. Wheels cream, striped in blue.

EQUIPMENT—As shown, including electric headlights. Electric spotlight on cowl. Electric horn. Dump bed operated by handle beside driver's seat.

WHEELS—10 x 1-inch R.T. disc.

WEIGHT—65 lbs. Packed set up for easy assembly, one in a crate.

No. 28-197—DUMP TRUCK

BODY—Length overall 52-inches. Width at pedals 12-inches.

FINISH—Body, hood and seat brown, striped and decorated in cream. Wheels cream, striped in brown.

EQUIPMENT—As shown, including high-speed gear (ratio 2 to 1). Gears revolving in lubricant in sealed housing unit. Electric head lights. Electric spotlight on cowl. Electric horn.

WHEELS—10 x 1-inch R. T. disc.

WEIGHT—75 lbs. Packed set up for easy assembly, one in a crate.

Gendron

No. 28-175

No. 28-177

SKIPPY FIRE DEPARTMENTS

No. 28-175—LADDER TRUCK

BODY—Length overall 51-inches. Width at pedals 14-inches.

FINISH—Body hood and seat red, striped in white. Wheels white, striped in red.

EQUIPMENT—As shown, including electric head lights, electric spotlight and siren.

WHEELS—10 x 1-inch rubber tire, artillery type.

WEIGHT—82 lbs. Packed set up for easy assembly, one in a crate.

No. 28-177—CHEMICAL

BODY—Length overall 51-inches. Width at pedals 12-inches.

FINISH—Body, hood and seat white, striped and decorated in red. Wheels red, striped in white.

EQUIPMENT—As shown, including ball bearing high speed propelling gear (ratio 2 to 1). Gears revolving in lubricant in sealed housing unit. Electric head lights. Electric spotlight. Instrument board.

WHEELS—10 x 1-inch rubber tire disc.

WEIGHT—90 lbs. Set up for easy assembly, one in a crate.

THE LINE THAT SETS THE PACE

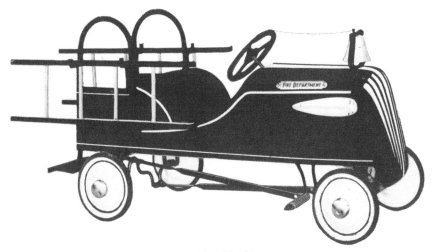

No. 28-171

No. 28-173

PIONEER LADDER TRUCKS

No. 28-171

BODY—Length overall 43-inches. Width at pedals 12-inches.

FINISH—Body, hood and seat red, striped in white. Wheels white, striped in red.

EQUIPMENT—As shown.

WHEELS—8 x ½-inch rubber tire disc.

WEIGHT—45 lbs. Packed K.D., one in a carton.

No. 28-173

BODY—Length overall 47-inches. Width at pedals 13-inches.

FINISH—Body, hood and seat red, striped in white. Wheels white, striped in red.

EQUIPMENT—As shown.

WHEELS—8 x ⅝-inch rubber tire artillery type.

WEIGHT—50 lbs. Packed K.D., one in a carton.

No. 28-155

No. 28-157

PIONEER FIRE CHIEFS

No. 28-155

(Patent Pending)

BODY—Length overall 36-inches. Width at pedals 13-inches.

FINISH—Body, hood and seat red, striped and decorated in aluminum. Wheels aluminum, striped in red.

EQUIPMENT—As shown.

FENDERS—Both front and rear fenders are an integral part of body.

WHEELS—8 x ½-inch rubber tire disc.

WEIGHT—37 lbs. Packed set up for easy assembly, one in a carton.

No. 28-157

(Patent Pending)

BODY—Length overall 39½-inches. Width at pedals 13-inches.

FINISH—Body, hood and seat red, striped and decorated in white. Wheels white, striped in red.

EQUIPMENT—As shown, including electric head lights.

FENDERS—Both front and rear fenders are an integral part of body.

WHEELS—8 x ⅝-inch rubber tire artillery type.

WEIGHT—38 pounds. Packed set up for easy assembly, one in a carton.

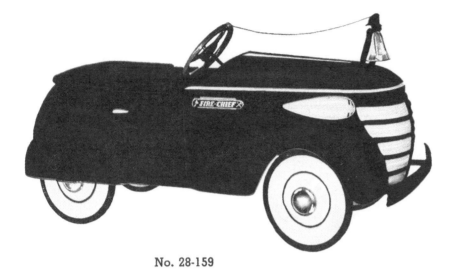

No. 28-159

No. 28-161

PIONEER FIRE CHIEFS

No. 28-159
(Patent Pending)

BODY—Length overall 45-inches. Width at pedals 14-

FINISH—Body, hood and seat red, striped and decorated in white. Wheels white, striped in red.

EQUIPMENT—As shown, including electric horn.

FENDERS—Both front and rear fenders are an integral part of body.

WHEELS—9½ x ⅝-inch rubber tire disc.

WEIGHT—60 lbs. Packed set up for easy assembly, one in a carton.

No. 28-161
(Patent Pending)

BODY—Length overall 47-inches. Width at pedals 14-inches.

FINISH—Body, hood and seat white, striped and decorated in red. Wheels white, striped in red.

EQUIPMENT—As shown, including ball bearing high speed gear (ratio 2 to 1). Gears revolving in lubricant in sealed housing unit. Electric horn and electric head lights.

WHEELS—9½ x ¾-inch rubber tire artillery type.

WEIGHT—62 lbs. Packed set up for easy assembly, one in a carton.

No. 28-151

No. 28-153

PIONEER FIRE CHIEFS

No. 28-151

BODY—Length overall 32-inches. Width at pedals 9-inches.

FINISH—Body, hood and seat red, striped and decorated in white. Wheels white, striped in red.

EQUIPMENT—As shown.

WHEELS—8 x ½-inch rubber tire disc.

WEIGHT—27 lbs. Packed K.D. one in a carton.

No. 28-153

BODY—Length overall 35-inches. Width at pedals 9½-inches.

FINISH—Body, hood and seat white enamel, striped and decorated in red. Wheels red, striped in white.

EQUIPMENT—As shown.

WHEELS—8 x ½-inch rubber tire artillery type.

WEIGHT—29 lbs. Packed K.D. one in a carton.

No. 28-127

No. 28-129

SKIPPY ROADSTERS

No. 28-127

BODY—Length overall 53-inches. Width at pedals 13-inches.

FINISH—Body, hood and seat red, striped and decorated in cream. Cream wheels, striped in red.

EQUIPMENT—As shown, including ball bearing high speed propelling gear (ratio 2 to 1). Gears revolving in lubricant in sealed housing unit. Electric head lights. Electric horn.

WHEELS—10 x 1-inch rubber tire artillery type.

WEIGHT—83 lbs. Packed set up for easy assembly, one in a crate.

No. 28-129

BODY—Length overall 53-inches. Width at pedals 13-inches.

FINISH—Body, hood and seat blue, striped and decorated in cream. Wheels cream enameled.

EQUIPMENT—As shown, including ball bearing high speed propelling gear (ratio 2 to 1). Gears revolving in lubricant in sealed housing unit. Electric horn. Electric head lights.

WHEELS—10 x 2-inch pneumatic tired ball bearing disc.

WEIGHT—83 lbs. Packed set up for easy assembly, one in a crate.

No. 28-123

No. 28-125

SKIPPY ROADSTERS

No. 28-123

BODY—Length overall 47-inches. Width at pedals 14-inches.

FINISH—Body, hood and seat cream, striped and decorated in red and black. Wheels cream. Fenders and dummy top black.

EQUIPMENT—As shown, including ball bearing high speed gear (ratio 2 to 1). Gears revolving in lubricant in sealed housing unit. Electric horn and head lights.

WHEELS—10 x 2-inch pneumatic tire, ball bearing disc.

WEIGHT—65 lbs. Packed set up for easy assembly, one in a carton.

No. 28-125

BODY—Length overall 53-inches. Width at pedals 13-inches.

FINISH—Maroon, striped and decorated in cream. Wheels cream, striped in maroon. Fenders and bumpers cream.

EQUIPMENT—As shown, including electric horn.

WHEELS—9½ x ¾-inch rubber tire artillery type.

WEIGHT—82 lbs. Packed set up for easy assembly, one in a crate.

Gendron

THE LINE THAT SETS THE PACE

No. 28-115

No. 28-117

PIONEER ROADSTERS

No. 28-115

(Patent Pending)

BODY—Length overall 45-inches. Width at pedals 14-inches.

FINISH—Body, hood and seat red, striped and decorated in cream. Wheels cream, striped in red.

FENDERS—Both front and rear fenders are an integral part of body.

EQUIPMENT—As shown, including electric horn.

WHEELS—9½ x ⅝-inch rubber tire disc.

WEIGHT—60 lbs. Packed set up for easy assembly, one in a carton.

No. 28-117

(Patent Pending)

BODY—Length overall 45-inches. Width at pedals 14-inches.

FINISH—Body, hood and seat brown, striped and decorated in cream. Wheels cream, striped in brown.

FENDERS—Both front and rear fenders are an integral part of body.

EQUIPMENT—As shown, including ball bearing high speed propelling gear (ratio 2 to 1). Gears revolving in lubricant in sealed housing unit. Electric horn.

WHEELS—9½ x ⅝-inch rubber tire artillery type.

WEIGHT—62 lbs. Packed set up for easy assembly, one in a carton.

No. 28-119

No. 28-121

PIONEER ROADSTERS

No. 28-119

BODY—Length overall 47-inches. Width at pedals 14-inches.

FINISH—Body, hood and seat green, striped and decorated in cream. Wheels green, striped in cream. Fenders cream.

EQUIPMENT—As shown, including ball bearing high speed propelling gear (ratio 2 to 1). Gears revolving in lubricant in sealed housing unit. Electric horn.

FENDERS—Both front and rear fenders are an integral part of body.

WHEELS—9½ x ¾-inch rubber tire artillery type.

WEIGHT—62 lbs. Packed set up for easy assembly, one in a carton.

No. 28-121

BODY—Length overall 47-inches. Width at pedals 14-inches.

FINISH—Body, hood and seat maroon, striped and decorated in red. Wheels red, striped in cream. Fenders and dummy top red.

EQUIPMENT—As shown, including ball bearing high speed propelling gear (ratio 2 to 1). Gears revolving in lubricant in sealed housing unit. Electric headlights. Electric horn.

FENDERS—Both front and rear fenders are an integral part of body.

WHEELS—10 x 1-inch rubber tire artillery type.

WEIGHT—65 lbs. Packed set up for easy assembly, one in a carton.

PIONEER LOCOMOTIVE

No. 28-139

BODY—Length overall 48-inches. Width at pedals 12-inches.

FINISH—Body red, trimmed in aluminum. Wheels, aluminum.

EQUIPMENT—As shown, including bell under cowl and electric head light.

WHEELS—9½ x ¾-inch rubber tire disc.

WEIGHT—81 lbs. Packed set up for easy assembly, one in a crate.

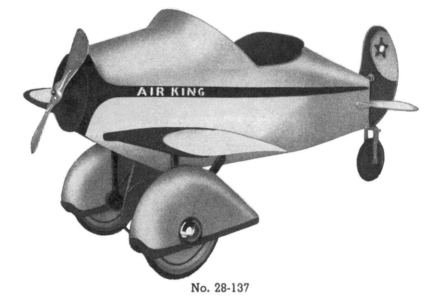

No. 28-137

No. 28-135

No. 28-135—SKIPPY AUTO TRAILER (ONLY)

BODY — Length overall 34-inches. Width 16-inches. Height 26-inches.

FINISH—Body silver aluminum, striped and decorated in green.

EQUIPMENT—As shown. Designed to accommodate one passenger. Seat in rear can be closed in rumble seat style when not in use. Coupling unit for towing connection. Window in front.

WHEELS—Front wheels 5 x ½-inch rubber tire disc. Rear wheels 9½ x ¾-inch rubber tire disc.

WEIGHT—40 lbs. Packed set up for easy assembly, one in a carton.

No. 28-137—AIR KING AIRPLANE

BODY—Length overall 50-inches. Width at pedals 13-inches. Wing spread 36-inches.

FINISH—Body lemon yellow, striped and decorated in green.

EQUIPMENT—As shown, with propeller which revolves when plane is in motion.

WHEELS—Front wheels 8 x ½-inch rubber tire disc. Rear wheel 5 x ½-inch rubber tire disc.

WEIGHT—44 pounds. Packed K.D., one in a carton.

No. 28-191

No. 28-193

No. 28-191—DUMP TRUCK

BODY—Length overall 45-inches. Width at pedals 12-inches.

FINISH—Body, hood and seat red, striped in cream. Dump box red. Wheels cream, striped in red.

EQUIPMENT—As shown, including dump bed operated by handle beside driver's seat.

WHEELS—8 x ½-inch R. T. disc.

WEIGHT—39 lbs. Packed K.D., one in a carton.

No. 28-193—DUMP TRUCK

BODY—Length overall 48-inches. Width at pedals 13-inches.

FINISH—Body, hood and seat green, striped in cream. Dump box cream enameled. Wheels cream enameled, striped in green.

EQUIPMENT—As shown, including dump box operated by handle beside driver's seat. Electric spotlight.

WHEELS—8 x ⅝-inch R. T. artillery.

WEIGHT—50 lbs. Packed K.D., one in a carton.

No. 28-101

No. 28-103

No. 28-105

PIONEER ROADSTERS

No. 28-101

BODY—Length overall 32-inches. Width at pedals 9-inches.

FINISH—Body, hood and seat green, striped and decorated in cream. Wheels cream, striped in green.

EQUIPMENT—As shown.

WHEELS—8 x ½-inch rubber tire disc.

WEIGHT—25 lbs. Packed K.D. one in a carton.

No. 28-103

BODY — Length overall 35-inches. Width at pedals 9½-inches.

FINISH—Body, hood and seat red, striped and decorated in cream. Wheels cream, striped in red.

EQUIPMENT—As shown.

WHEELS—8 x ½-inch rubber tire artillery type.

WEIGHT—29 lbs. Packed K. D. one in a carton.

No. 28-105

BODY—Length overall 35-inches. Width at pedals 9½-inches.

FINISH—Body, hood and seat brown, striped and decorated in cream. Wheels cream, striped in brown.

EQUIPMENT—As shown.

WHEELS—8 x ½-inch rubber tire artillery type.

WEIGHT—31 lbs. Packed K. D. one in a carton.

No. 28-107

No. 28-109

PIONEER ROADSTERS

No. 28-107

(Patent Pending)

BODY—Length overall 36-inches. Width at pedals 13-inches.

FINISH—Body, hood and seat green, striped and decorated in aluminum. Wheels aluminum, striped in green.

EQUIPMENT—As shown.

FENDERS—Both front and rear fenders are an integral part of body.

WHEELS—8 x ½-inch rubber tire disc.

WEIGHT—36 lbs. Packed set up for easy assembly, one in a carton.

No. 28-109

(Patent Pending)

BODY—Length overall 36-inches. Width at pedals 13-inches.

FINISH—Body, hood and seat red, striped and decorated in cream. Wheels cream, striped in red.

EQUIPMENT—As shown.

FENDERS—Both front and rear fenders are an integral part of body.

WHEELS—8 x ½-inch rubber tire artillery type.

WEIGHT—37 lbs. Packed set up for easy assembly, one in a carton.

No. 28-111

No. 28-113

PIONEER ROADSTERS

No. 28-111
(Patent Pending)

BODY—Length overall 39½-inches. Width at pedals 13-inches.

FINISH—Body, hood and seat Lincoln Blue, striped and decorated in cream. Wheels cream, striped in blue.

EQUIPMENT—As shown, including electric horn.

FENDERS—Both front and rear fenders are an integral part of body.

WHEELS—8 x ½-inch rubber tired disc.

WEIGHT—38 lbs. Packed set up for easy assembly, one in a carton.

No. 28-113
(Patent Pending)

BODY—Length overall 39½-inches. Width at pedals 13-inches.

FINISH—Body, hood and seat cream, striped and decorated in red. Wheels cream, striped in red. Fenders and dummy top red.

EQUIPMENT—As shown, including electric horn.

FENDERS—Both front and rear fenders are an integral part of body.

WHEELS—8 x ⅝-inch rubber tired artillery type.

WEIGHT—39 lbs. Packed set up for easy assembly, one in a carton.

No. 20-110

© P. L. CROSBY

This model equipped with red enameled imitation top as on No. 20-118.

No. 20-112

PIONEER AND SKIPPY ROADSTERS
Patent No. 2,145,896

No. 20-110
BODY—Length overall 40-inches. Hood is raised and lowered as illustrated. Imitation motor under hood.

FINISH—Body blue, striped and decorated in grey. Hood grey. Wheels grey, striped in blue.

EQUIPMENT—As shown. WHEELS—8 x ⅝-inch rubber tire artillery type, helical steel bearings.

No. 20-109
Exactly the same as No. 20-110 above except less the imitation motor under the hood. Finished in maroon, trimmed in red, striped in cream. Hood red.

No. 20-112
BODY—Length overall 40-inches. Hood is raised and lowered as illustrated. Imitation motor under hood.

WHEELS—8 x ⅝-inch rubber tire artillery type, helical steel bearings.

WEIGHT—39 pounds. Packed one in a carton.

FINISH—Body cream, striped and decorated in red. Hood red. Wheels red, striped in cream.

EQUIPMENT—As shown, including electric horn.

No. 20-099

No. 20-100
Designed by Brooks Stevens

© P. L. CROSBY

No. 20-104   Designed by Brooks Stevens

PIONEER AND SKIPPY ROADSTERS

No. 20-099

BODY—Length 32-inches.

FINISH—Body, hood and seat red, striped and decorated in cream. Wheels cream, striped in red.

EQUIPMENT—As shown.

WHEELS—8 x ½-inch rubber tire disc, helical steel bearings.

WEIGHT—25 lbs. Packed K.D. one in a carton.

No. 20-100

BODY—Length 34¼-inches.

FINISH—Body, hood and seat green, striped and decorated in yellow. Wheels yellow, striped in green.

EQUIPMENT—As shown.

WHEELS—8 x ½-inch rubber tire disc, helical steel bearings.

WEIGHT—25 pounds. Packed K.D. one in a carton.

No. 20-104

BODY—Length 34¼-inches.

FINISH—Body, hood and seat blue, striped and decorated in cream. Wheels cream, striped in blue.

EQUIPMENT—As shown.

WHEELS—8 x ½-inch rubber tire artillery type, helical steel bearings.

WEIGHT—29 pounds. Packed K.D. one in a carton.

PAGE THIRTY-SEVEN

Gendron

NOTE—Electric spotlight shown on cowl discontinued.

© P. L. CROSBY

No. 20-179

No. 20-183

No. 20-179—SKIPPY HOSE CART

BODY—Length overall 56-inches. Width at pedals 12-inches.

FINISH—Body, hood and seat red, striped and decorated in white. Wheels red, striped in white.

EQUIPMENT—As shown, including ball bearing high speed gear (ratio 2 to 1). Gears revolving in lubricant in sealed housing unit. Electric headlights. Rubber hose with nozzle and hydrant attachment. Siren.

WHEELS—10 x 1½-inch moulded rubber tire, artillery type, full floating helical steel bearings.

WEIGHT—90 lbs. Packed set up for easy assembly, one in a crate.

No. 20-183—SKIPPY RACER

BODY—Length overall 55-inches. Width at pedals 12-inches.

FINISH—Body, hood and seat red, striped and decorated in aluminum. Wheels white.

EQUIPMENT—As shown, including ball bearing high speed gear (ratio 2 to 1). Gears revolving in lubricant in sealed housing unit. Electric horn.

WHEELS—10 x 2¾-inch pneumatic tire, ball bearing disc.

WEIGHT—70 lbs. Packed set up for easy assembly, one in a crate.

PAGE FORTY-EIGHT

115

No. 20-191

No. 20-193

PIONEER DUMP TRUCKS

No. 20-191

BODY—Length overall 45-inches. Width at pedals 12-inches.

FINISH—Body, hood and seat red, striped in cream. Dump box red. Wheels cream, striped in red.

EQUIPMENT—As shown, including dump bed operated by handle beside driver's seat.

WHEELS—8 x ½-inch R. T. disc, full floating helical steel bearings.

WEIGHT—39 lbs. Packed K.D., one in a carton.

No. 20-193

BODY—Length overall 48-inches. Width at pedals 13-inches.

FINISH—Body, hood and seat green, striped in cream. Dump box cream enameled. Wheels cream enameled, striped in green.

EQUIPMENT—As shown, including dump box operated by handle beside driver's seat.

WHEELS—8 x ⅝-inch R. T. artillery, full floating helical steel bearings.

WEIGHT—50 lbs. Packed K.D., one in a carton.

PAGE FORTY-NINE

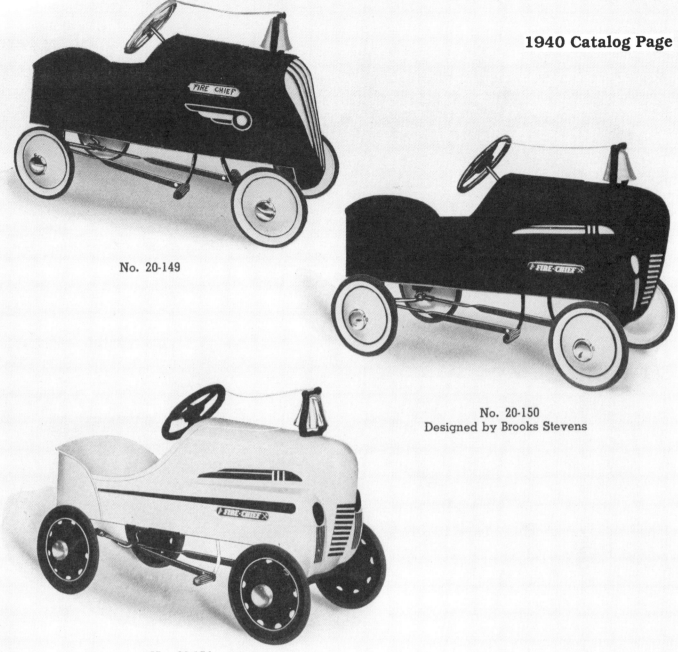

No. 20-149

No. 20-150
Designed by Brooks Stevens

No. 20-154
Designed by Brooks Stevens

PIONEER FIRE CHIEFS

No. 20-149

BODY—Length 32-inches.
FINISH—Body, hood and seat red, striped and decorated in white. Wheels white, striped in red.
EQUIPMENT—As shown.
WHEELS—8 x ½-inch rubber tire disc, helical steel bearings.
WEIGHT—27 pounds. Packed K.D. one in a carton.

No. 20-150

BODY—Length 34¼-inches.
FINISH—Body, hood and seat red, striped and decorated in white. Wheels white, striped in red.
EQUIPMENT—As shown.
WHEELS—8 x ½-inch rubber tire disc, helical steel bearings.
WEIGHT—27 pounds. Packed K.D. one in a carton.

No. 20-154

BODY—Length 34¼-inches.
FINISH—Body, hood and seat white enamel, striped and decorated in red. Wheels red, striped in white.
EQUIPMENT—As shown.
WHEELS—8 x ½-inch rubber tire artillery type, helical steel bearings.
WEIGHT—27 pounds. Packed K.D. one in a carton.

PAGE FORTY-FOUR

No. 20-156

No. 20-158

PIONEER FIRE CHIEFS
Patent No. 2,145,896

No. 20-156

BODY—Length overall 37-inches. Hood is raised and lowered as illustrated.

FINISH—Body and hood red, striped and decorated in white. Wheels white, striped in red.

EQUIPMENT—As shown.

WHEELS—8 x ½-inch rubber tire disc, helical steel bearings.

WEIGHT—37 pounds. Packed one in a carton.

No. 20-158

BODY—Length overall 40-inches. Hood is raised and lowered as illustrated. Imitation motor under hood.

FINISH—Body white, striped and decorated in red. Hood red. Wheels red, striped in white.

EQUIPMENT—As shown.

WHEELS—8 x ⅝-inch rubber tire artillery type, helical steel bearings.

WEIGHT—38 pounds. Packed one in a carton.

PAGE FORTY-FIVE

Gendron

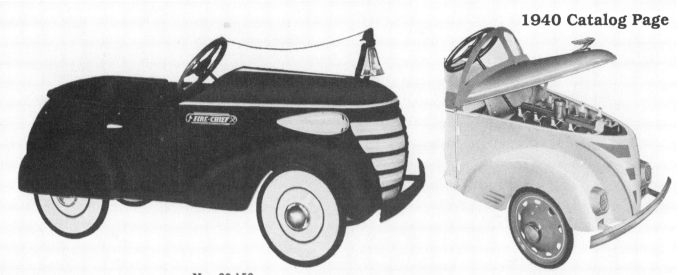

No. 20-159

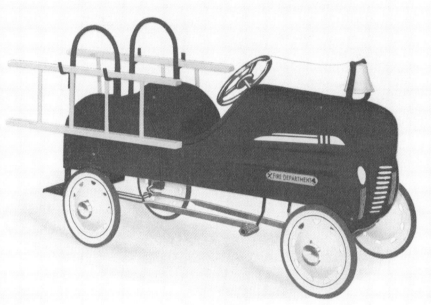

No. 20-172

PIONEER FIRE EQUIPMENT

No. 20-159

BODY—Length overall 45-inches. Hood is raised and lowered as illustrated. Imitation motor under hood.

FINISH—Body red, striped and decorated in white. Hood white. Wheels white, striped in red.

EQUIPMENT—As shown, including electric horn.

WHEELS—9½ x ⅝-inch rubber tire disc, helical steel bearings.

WEIGHT—52 pounds. Packed one in a carton.

No. 20-172

BODY—Length overall 51-inches.

FINISH—Body, hood and seat red, striped and decorated in white. Wheels white, striped in red.

EQUIPMENT—As shown.

WHEELS—8 x ½-inch rubber tire artillery type helical steel bearings.

WEIGHT—45 pounds. Packed K.D. one in a carton.

No. 20-174

© P. L. CROSBY

No. 20-175

SKIPPY LADDER TRUCKS

| No. 20-174 | No. 20-175 |

No. 20-174

BODY—Length overall 47-inches.

FINISH—Body and hood red, striped and decorated in white. Wheels white, striped in red.

EQUIPMENT—As shown.

WHEELS—8 x ⅝-inch rubber tire artillery type, helical steel bearings.

WEIGHT—50 pounds. Packed one in a carton.

No. 20-175

BODY—Length overall 51-inches. Hood is raised and lowered as illustrated. Imitation motor under hood.

FINISH—Body red, striped and decorated in white. Hood white. Wheels white, striped in red.

EQUIPMENT—As shown.

WHEELS—10 x 1-inch rubber tire artillery type, helical steel bearings.

WEIGHT—76 pounds. Packed set up for easy assembly, one in a crate.

PAGE FORTY-SEVEN

Gendron

No. 20-116

No. 20-118

PIONEER AND SKIPPY ROADSTERS
Patent No. 2,145,896

No. 20-116

BODY—Length overall 45-inches. Hood is raised and lowered as illustrated. Imitation motor under hood.

FINISH—Body red, striped and decorated in cream. Hood maroon. Wheels cream, striped in red.

EQUIPMENT—As shown.

WHEELS—9½ x ⅝-inch rubber tire disc, helical steel bearings.

WEIGHT—51 pounds. Packed one in a carton.

No. 20-118

BODY—Length overall 45-inches. Hood is raised and lowered as illustrated. Imitation motor under hood.

FINISH—Body blue, striped and decorated in aluminum. Hood aluminum. Wheels aluminum, striped in blue.

EQUIPMENT—As shown, including electric horn.

WHEELS—9½ x ¾-inch rubber tire artillery type, helical steel bearings.

WEIGHT—54 pounds. Packed one in a carton.

PAGE FORTY

121

No. 20-120

© P. L. CROSBY

No. 20-122

PIONEER AND SKIPPY ROADSTERS
Patent No. 2,145,896

No. 20-120

BODY—Length overall 47-inches. Hood is raised and lowered as illustrated. Imitation motor under hood.

FINISH—Body iridescent green, striped in red and decorated in white. Dark green hood and dummy top. Wheels white, striped in green.

EQUIPMENT—As shown, including ball-bearing high-speed propelling gear (ratio 2 to 1), electric horn.

WHEELS—9½ x ¾-inch rubber tire artillery type, helical steel bearings.

WEIGHT—58 pounds. Packed one in a carton.

No. 20-122

BODY—Length overall 47-inches. Hood is raised and lowered as illustrated. Imitation motor under hood.

FINISH—Body mist grey, striped and decorated in red. Hood mist grey with large red panel. Wheels grey, striped in red.

EQUIPMENT—As shown, including ball-bearing high-speed propelling gear (ratio 2 to 1), electric horn.

WHEELS—10 x 1-inch rubber tire artillery type, helical steel bearings.

WEIGHT—60 pounds. Packed one in a carton.

PAGE FORTY-ONE

Gendron

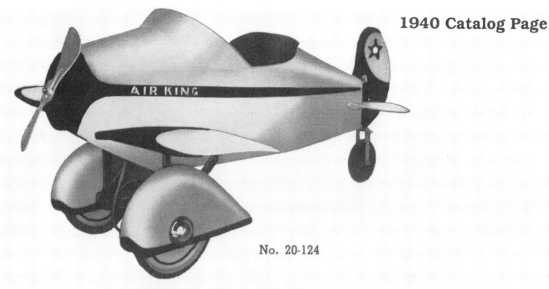

No. 20-124

No. 20-124—AIR KING AIRPLANE

BODY—Length overall 50-inches. Width at pedals 13-inches. Wing spread 36-inches.

FINISH—Body aluminum, striped and decorated in red.

EQUIPMENT—As shown, with propeller which revolves when plane is in motion.

WHEELS—Front wheels 8 x ½-inch rubber tire disc. Rear wheel 5 x ½-inch rubber tire disc, full floating helical steel bearings.

WEIGHT—44 pounds. Packed K.D., one in a carton.

ADDITIONAL PLAY VALUE

Here is a graphic illustration of how children can enjoy the opening hoods and imitation motors which we use on the majority of our juvenile automobiles for 1940.

Gendron

PAGE FORTY-TWO

© P L. CROSBY

No. 20-125

No. 20-129

SKIPPY ROADSTERS

No. 20-125

BODY—Length overall 53-inches. Width at pedals 13-inches.

FINISH—Maroon, striped and decorated in cream. Wheels cream, striped in maroon. Fenders and bumpers cream.

EQUIPMENT—As shown, including electric horn and ball bearing drive rods.

WHEELS—9½ x ¾-inch rubber tire artillery type, helical steel bearings.

WEIGHT—82 lbs. Packed set up for easy assembly, one in a crate.

No. 20-129

BODY—Length overall 53-inches. Width at pedals 13-inches.

FINISH—Body, hood and seat blue, striped and decorated in cream. Wheels cream enameled.

EQUIPMENT—As shown, including ball bearing high speed propelling gear (ratio 2 to 1). Gears revolving in lubricant in sealed housing unit. Electric horn. Electric head lights.

WHEELS—10 x 2-inch pneumatic tired ball bearing disc.

WEIGHT—83 lbs. Packed set up for easy assembly, one in a crate.

PAGE FORTY-THREE

Gendron

No. 20-106

No. 20-108

© P. L. CROSBY

PIONEER AND SKIPPY ROADSTERS
Patent No. 2,145,896

No. 20-106

BODY—Length overall 37-inches. Hood is raised and lowered as illustrated.

FINISH—Body mist grey, striped and decorated in red with red hood. Wheels red, striped in grey.

EQUIPMENT—As shown.

WHEELS—8 x ½-inch rubber tire disc, helical steel bearings.

WEIGHT—36 pounds. Packed one in a carton.

No. 20-108

BODY—Length overall 37-inches. Hood is raised and lowered as illustrated.

FINISH—Body red, striped and decorated in mist grey. Hood mist grey. Wheels grey, striped in red.

EQUIPMENT—As shown.

WHEELS—8 x ½-inch rubber tire artillery type, helical steel bearings.

WEIGHT—37 pounds. Packed one in a carton.

PAGE THIRTY-EIGHT

Gendron

SPACE CRUISER

7200

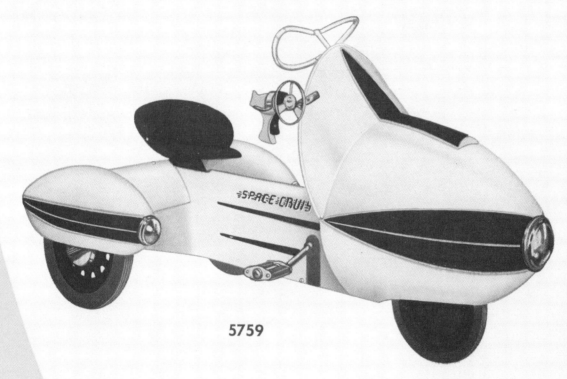

5759

5759 — SPACE CRUISER

BODY — Length overall 48 inches. Width 27 inches.

FINISH — White, decorated red and yellow.

GEAR — Speedy, easy to operate chain drive. Ball bearings on rear axle and pedal crank.

WHEELS — Rear wheels 10 x 1.75 inches molded tire with nylon bearings. Front wheel 8 x 1.25 molded tire with nylon bearings.

STEERING MECHANISM — Swivel type front wheel (nylon bearing stem) permits 360° turning through universal joint attached to steering rod.

EQUIPMENT — Flying saucer gun that really shoots. Two way adjustable safety type bucket saddle to allow use by wider age range children.

PACKING — One in carton.

WEIGHT — 51 pounds.

7200 — SLED GUARD

SIZE — Length 14 inches, width 13 inches, height 9½ inches.

CONSTRUCTION — Collapsible to fit any sled our make. Made of seasoned hardwood and heavy gauge strip steel.

FINISH — Wood parts varnished natural. Steel strip enameled in red.

PACKING — ½ dozen in carton.

WEIGHT — 21 pounds per carton.

G A R T O N   T O Y   C O M P A N Y   •

1956 Magazine Ad

how to play Santa with an *easy mind*

More presents under the Christmas tree! You can spend more for family fun — once you have Mutual of Omaha's "Easy Mind" insurance. Relax and spend happily — with the knowledge that you are insured, as millions are, by Mutual of Omaha, largest company in the world specializing in health and accident insurance.

MUTUAL OF OMAHA
"easy mind" Health Insurance

DON'T WAIT...UNTIL IT'S TOO LATE...MAIL COUPON NOW!

1962 Magazine Ad

About your family cars and Securance. Securance can't keep a shine on your chrome, but it *can* provide you with the last word in driving protection—through Nationwide Insurance, the choice of over 2¼ million careful drivers. You get broad coverage—as liberal as any anywhere—at fair rates, backed by claims service that's really *fast*. Yet quality car insurance is only *part* of your Securance "package." Securance can also insure your *life, health, family, home* and *property*. All at low cost, with no gaps, overlaps or extras. All through your Nationwide agent, who takes care of all the details for you. Check your Yellow Pages for his name and number.

Securance is all-risk, one agent, "packaged" protection. Covers your life, health, home, car and property. It's available only through your Nationwide agent. He's in the Yellow Pages.

1920 Magazine Ad

WHAT'S HE WORTH
TO HIS TOWN?

IS this budding taxpayer of enough value as a prospective citizen to deserve all the odds in his favor to reach a happy, healthy manhood?

Here is a public matter to put every thinking man and woman to the test.

The boy's most precious property is his good health. He needs for the preservation of this good health, a clean town to grow up in, a town free from flies, mosquitoes, typhoid fever, bad drainage and bad air. He needs a good home with baths and plumbing in it.

The United States Public Health Service tells us that "typhoid fever, the dysenteries, hookworm disease, much of the diarrhea of infant and adult life and much of the tuberculosis, are preventable by the installation of a complete sewer system reaching all premises."

The first essential of such a system of sanitation is that it be capable of rendering for generations a healthful service to the community.

That is the certainty which only Vitrified Clay Sanitary Sewer Pipe can afford.

Uniformly factory-made and infallibly tested by fire, its quality is a certainty before laying.

Certainty to withstand unceasing attack by destructive agents in sewage and in soil, and certainty to be forever dense, never menacing health by seepage, are other important and exclusive attributes of Vitrified Clay Pipe.

Lay it sure with Vitrified Clay!

And do it now. The cost of sanitation can never exceed the value of little lives.

CLAY PRODUCTS ASSOCIATION
CHICAGO   PITTSBURGH

VITRIFIED CLAY
Sanitary Sewer Pipe

1927 Magazine Ad

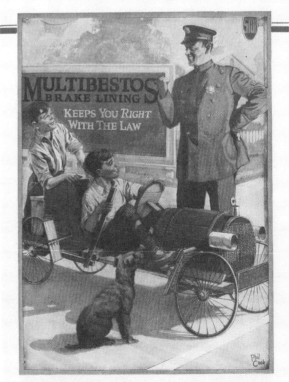

Have this Picture on your Wall or Window

DEALERS and Service Stations: Write for a large size copy of this picture, printed in four colors, size 22 by 28 inches. Free. Makes a striking window display. Is equally attractive hung on your wall. Address Department M. —

MULTIBESTOS COMPANY, WALPOLE, MASS., U. S. A.

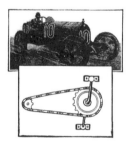

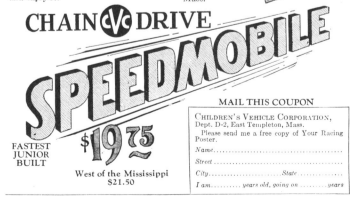

MAKE-BELIEVE is fun!

...but NOT when buying shoes for growing feet—
Make sure your children's shoes are right!

STANDARD ...Too, in the
Great American Motor Industry

PHOTOGRAPHS COURTESY STUDEBAKER CORPORATION OF AMERICA

An accurate machining operation   *Inspectors testing motor horsepower*   *The smiling service man*

Hidden values make the difference between shoes that are *right* for growing feet and shoes that *look* right when new but soon lose their shape.

You can't see the hidden values in any child's shoe. But they are the secret to longer wear and lasting fit . . . *better fitting lasts* . . . *best materials available* . . . *expert workmanship* . . . *plus extra reinforcements* in the *hidden parts* as

well as in parts you can see!

That's why it pays to insist on children's shoes with the name WEATHER-BIRD or PETERS DIAMOND BRAND *stamped in the shoe.* Either name *guarantees* the best value, through and through, that more than fifty years of quality shoemaking experience can put in a shoe.

Peters, Branch of International Shoe Company, St. Louis, Mo.

THE QUALITY IS THERE IN EVERY PAIR

KEEN, capable men in Lee Overalls build the cars and trucks in America's great motor car plants. Keen, capable men in Lee Union-Alls lettered with the greatest names of motordom give smiling service for thousands of motor car dealers throughout America.

In the motor industry, as elsewhere
▼ ▼ ▼ ▼ ▼

THE H. D. LEE MERCANTILE COMPANY
KANSAS CITY MINNEAPOLIS TRENTON SOUTH BEND
SALINA SAN FRANCISCO

A great American Organization enjoying an International Business

throughout America, the name Lee is great because more Lee Overalls and Lee Union-Alls are worn than work clothing of any other make. "Lee . . . The World's Standard" is the reward in popularity bestowed by millions of American men with pride in their jobs".

THE WORLD'S STANDARD
Lee OVERALLS
UNION-ALLS
PLAY SUITS

What the WEATHER-BIRD
standard of value means to you

1. **LONGER WEAR**—best materials available . . . expert workmanship . . . plus extra reinforcements in *hidden parts*, as well as in parts you can see.
2. **LASTING FIT** — because Weather-Birds hold their shape and thus keep their fit longer.
3. **FOOT-FORMED LASTS** — ample toe room and heels of the right height help growing feet *develop normally.*
4. **COMFORTABLE FLEXIBILITY** — due to exclusive manufacturing processes and construction features.
5. **AUTHENTIC STYLES**—for every purpose—every purse.

WEATHER-BIRD
and Peters Diamond Brand
SHOES FOR BOYS AND GIRLS
Help Uncle Sam—Buy U. S. War Bonds and Stamps

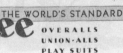

PETER NEVE RIDES OUT IN HIS CHRISTMAS PRESENT

You can depend on your Doctor of Motors

PERFECT CIRCLE
Custom Made Piston Ring Sets

PISTON RINGS — PISTON NURLIZING
MANULATHE -- PLASTIGAGE - BEARING ADJUSTERS

"Parts Headquarters for the Doctor of Motors"

AUGUST 1950

SUN	MON	TUE	WED	THU	FRI	SAT
LAST QUAR. 5d.	NEW MOON 13d.	1	2	3	4	5
6	7	8	9	10	11	12
13	14	15	16	17	18	19
20	21	22	23	24	25	26
27	28	29	30	31	FIRST QUAR. 20th	FULL MOON 27th

JULY 1950						
SUN	MON	TUE	WED	THU	FRI	SAT
						1
2	3	4	5	6	7	8
9	10	11	12	13	14	15
16	17	18	19	20	21	22
23 30	24 31	25	26	27	28	29

SEPTEMBER 1950						
SUN	MON	TUE	WED	THU	FRI	SAT
					1	2
3	4	5	6	7	8	9
10	11	12	13	14	15	16
17	18	19	20	21	22	23
24	25	26	27	28	29	30

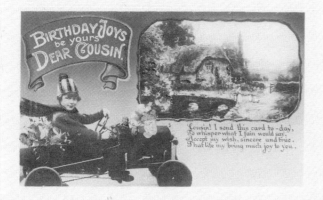

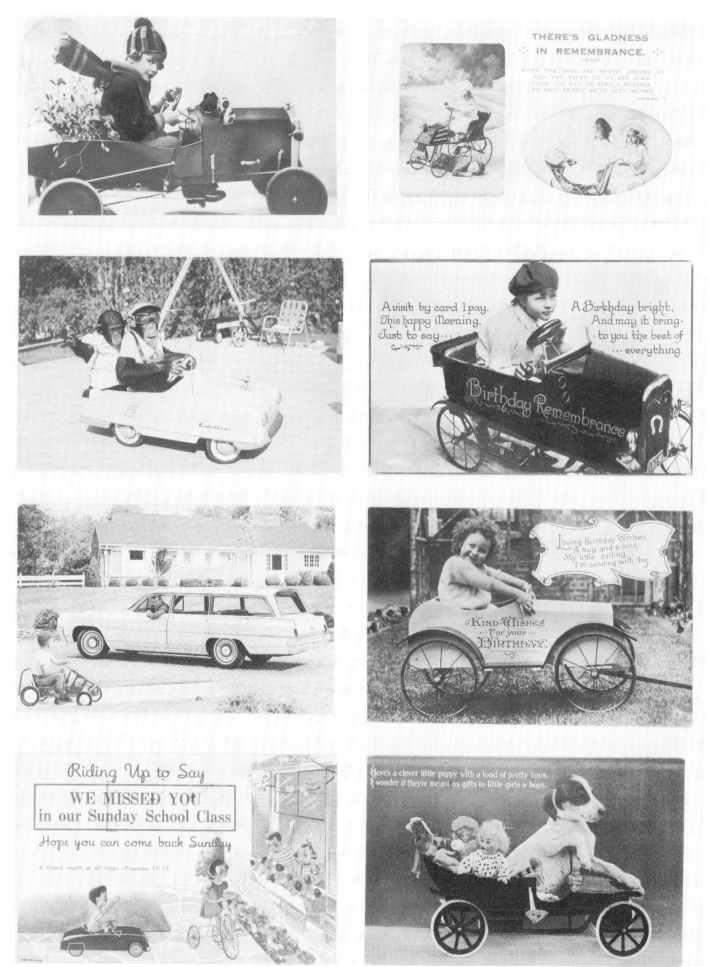

CLEAR THE WAY!

In our breezy easy motor,
We've come over for a run,
With a load of loving wishes
And a moverfull of fun.

EXPECT ME SHORTLY—
COMING IN MY RACING AUTO.

All Birthday Joys be Yours.

Fond is the greeting,
I'm sending to say,
Good Luck to you, dear,
And a joyous Birthday.

TO WISH YOU A MERRY CHRISTMAS.

All sweet memories of the past unite
With present joys to make your Christmas bright.

Upon My Soul (Sole) I'd Rather Walk.

Actual Photograph

1925 Actual Photograph of Harold Lenz Age 3 1/2

Actual Postcard

ctual Photograph 1924 Toledo Lincoln

143

Actual Photograph of 1930 Steelcraft

Actual Photograph of Late 1910's to Early 1920's Pedal Car

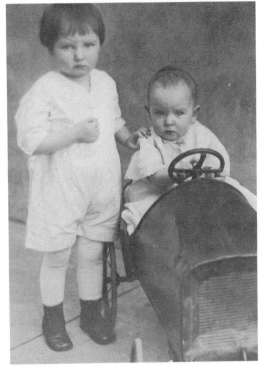

Actual Photograph of 1920 American National

Photograph of David M. Leopard with his father

1936 Actual Photograph

1930's Maker Unknown
Driver Yvonne
Marc Hagervan
The Netherlands

1932 Steelcraft
Melvin Vesely
LaGrange Park,IL

1908 Torck' Belgium
Fritz Erckens
Krämerstrabe 23,Deutschland

1952 Murray
Daniel Karpinen
Queens,NY

1929 Steelcraft Auburn
Pat Guiney
Nashua,NH

1932 Cadillac
Driver Jan Mowery
Lincoln,NE

1950 Murray Station Wagon
Dennis Dickson
Lebanon,OR

Late 1910's-Maker Unknown
O.S.Ebersole
Hummelstown,PA

150

1958 Murray Champion
Daniel Rocha in Ray's (Big Brother) Car
Ray Rocha
Omaha,NE

1941 Steelcraft Chrysler
Jim Smith
Garland,TX

1928 Steelcraft
Peter Torres
Granada Hill,CA

1945 Murray
Peter Torres
Granada Hill,CA

1949 Garton Station Wagon
The Bennett Family
Kevin Bennett
Zillah,WA

Mid 1940's Murray's
Drivers-Richard Geary & Jim Geary
Jim Geary
Goldsboro,NC

1934 Steelcraft Mack
Betty Klang
Tacoma,WA

1968 Calendar

MARSHALL COUNTY BUILDING &
LOAN ASSN.
201 N. MICHIGAN ST. — PHONE 936-2524
PLYMOUTH, IND.

Magazine Cover

Magazine Cover

Magazine Cover

NELSONS FEED STORE
DEALER IN FLOUR, FEED, SEEDS
and BINDER TWINE
GRINDING and MIXING
WE MANUFACTURE OUR OWN POULTRY MASHES
BALSAM LAKE, WISCONSIN

1938		MARCH			1938	
SUN	MON	TUE	WED	THU	FRI	SAT
		1	2	3	4	5
6	7	8	9	10	11	12
13	14	15	16	17	18	19
20	21	22	23	24	25	26
27	28	29	30	31		

MOTHER HUBBARD FLOUR

NELSON'S FEED STORE
FEEDS MASHES
Made the HUBBARD SUNSHINE Way

"WHY DON'T YOU LEARN TO DRIVE?"

Sioux City Serum Company

SIOUX BRAND SERUM

U. S. VETERINARY LICENSE No. 37
PIONEER PRODUCER OF POTENT SERUM AND VIRULENT VIRUS

December						1917
Sun	Mon	Tues	Wed	Thu	Fri	Sat
						1
2	3	4	5	6	7	8
9	10	11	12	13	14	15
16	17	18	19	20	21	22
23 30	24 31	25	26	27	28	29

SIOUX

CITY

IOWA

January						1918
Sun	Mon	Tues	Wed	Thu	Fri	Sat
		1	2	3	4	5
6	7	8	9	10	11	12
13	14	15	16	17	18	19
20	21	22	23	24	25	26
27	28	29	30	31		

TELEPHONES:

OFFICE BELL 190
AUTO 4604

AFTER 6 P. M.
BELL 2489   AUTO 5717
"   939   "   4727
"   6650
"   6731

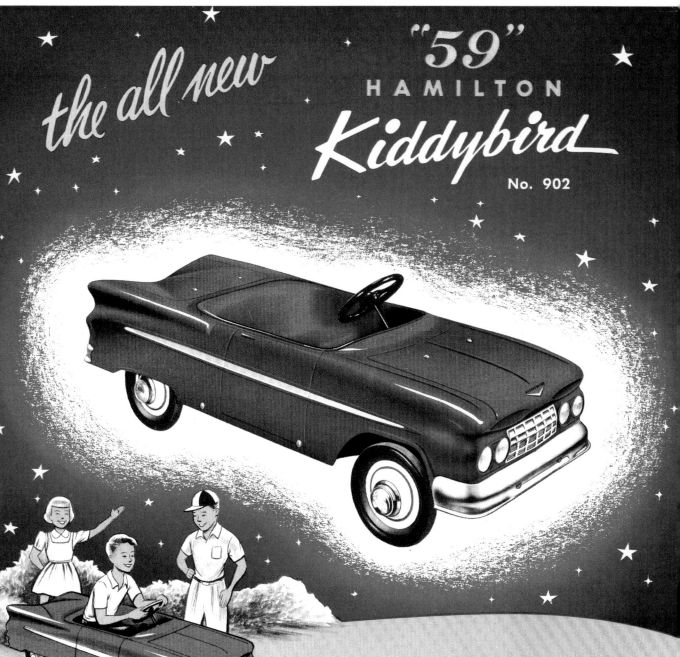

the all new **"59"**

HAMILTON

Kiddybird

No. 902

dream of the junior set

**Rear view of the beautiful "59" Kiddybird.
Outstanding styling in colorful plastic.**

NO. 902 KIDDYBIRD

The new 1959 Kiddybird design and style is indeed the dream of every youngster. "Just like dad's new car!" The sculptured all plastic body is securely mounted on a rugged all steel channel constructed frame. Chain drive and easy steering for top performance. Packed one to carton. Shipping wt. 43 lbs.

SPECIFICATIONS

- All plastic body
- Steel channel constructed frame
- Wheels 1¼" x 8"
- Semi-pneumatic auto-type tires
- Chain drive and easy steering
- 50" long — 21" wide — 43 lbs.
- Trade marked

HAMILTON STEEL PRODUCTS, INC.
1845 WEST 74TH STREET • CHICAGO 36, ILLINOIS

THE NEXT 22 PAGES
FURNISHED BY:

ELMER DUELLMAN
FOUNTAIN CITY, WI

Elmer is one of the largest collectors of Pedal Cars in the world. He also collects Antique & Classic Cars, Toys, Bicycles, Motorcycles and many other antiques & collectables. Without his help and encouragement this book or volume #1 & #2 could not have been completed

ELMER THANKS A MILLION

The Editor
Neil S. Wood

1936 Steelcraft Chevy

1959 Murray with Original Radio

**1970's Thunderbird "Cherry 7up"
Made by Bird Co.(Plastic)**

1950's Murray Firetruck

1960 Garton Firetruck

**1935 Steelcraft Auburn
Restored**

1938 Steelcraft Dodge

1949 Triang-England Race Car

1925 Steelcraft Cleveland Original

Early 1970's Lambourgini

1928 Steelcraft Lincoln

1926 Steelcraft

1912 Gendron Race Car

1914 American National Ace Race Car

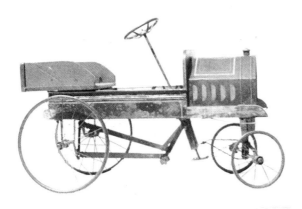

1908 Gendron Race Car

1910's American National Ace Race Car

1908 Cadillac

1870 Three-Wheeler

Late 1930's Tool Box "Tow & Fix It"

1923 Gendron Cadillac Original

1970 Garton Little Princess Original

1941 Steelcraft Chrysler Fire Chief

1925 American National Lincoln

1934 Steelcraft Skippy Original

1937 Toledo Skippy Pontiac

1925 Steelcraft

1936 Garton Zephyr Deluxe

**1959 Murray Firetruck
Original Key in Ignition**

1959 Murray Dude Wagon

1940 Garton Fire Chief Original

1932 Gendron Lincoln

1934 Garton Buick

1939 Pal Dumptruck

1935 Steelcraft Pontiac

1961 Murray "Dr.Pepper"

1915 Race Car

1935 Toledo Skippy DeSoto

1955 Murray Champion

1948 Steger Firetruck

Trike with Side Car

1932 Steelcraft Buick

**1920's AMF Hi-Ball Hand Car
Chain Drive**

1934 Steelcraft Cadillac

1952 BMC Firetruck

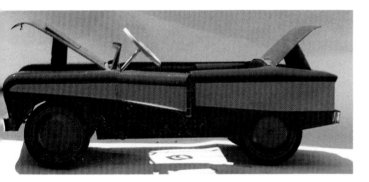

1964 Argentina Falcon

1953 BMC Studebaker Jet Hawk

Late 1940's Garton Tank

1922 Gendron Dumptruck

1938 LaSalle Skippy

1949 Garton Fire Chief

1929 Gendron's

1950's Murray Wrecker

1924 Steelcraft Studebaker

1941 Steelcraft Auburn

1986 Corvette Pace Car

1949 Murray Fire Chief

1991 Race Car
Made by Miracle Pedal Car Co.

1937 Steelcraft Airflow

1938 Garton LaSalle

1970's Ertel Pontiac
Richard Petty-Ride On

**1935 Steelcraft "G-Man Cruiser"
with Original Gun**

1922 Gendron "Willy's-Knight"

Hand Made by Ron Doan

**1921 CBC Speedmobile Car
Chain Drive**

1968 Camaro Hand Made

**1952 Murray Skipper
All Original Motor**

1952 Murray Atomic Missle

1924 Steelcraft Chief of Police

**Hand Made Wrecker
Made by Ron Doan**

1926 American National Buick

Hand Made Packard Coupe

Late 1950's Garton Mark V

**1924 Gendron Race Car
Sprocket Drive**

**1958 Hamilton Chevy
Fiberglass-Chain Drive**

**Late 1940's Murray
Happitime Firetruck**

**1926 American National
"Curtis Tanager"**

Late 1960's Garton Probe X

**1951 Garton Kidillac
Original**

Late 1940's Austin Race Car

1934 Steelcraft Pontiac

1926 American National Buick
Originally on Barber Chair
Trunk was for Barber's Tools

All the Pictures on this Page are a 1932 American National Firetruck

1990 Thunderbird (Plastic)

1930 Steelcraft Skippy

1923 American National Marmon

1934 Gendron Race Car
"Wilber Shaw"

1931 Steelcraft & 1936 Steelcraft

1952 BMC Race Car's

Mid 1950's Jeep (All Aluminum) & 1938 Steelcraft Oldsmobile

1965 Murray Mustang's

1952 Custom BMC Race Car

1958 Chevy Impala By Hamilton
This Was the First Real Automobile That Elmer
Bought, Which He Still Owns.

1952 Kidillac Custom
Lowered, Cruiser Skirts, Sidepipes, Wirewheels
and a Custom Paint

1920's American National Lone Eagle

Original Truck By AMF
Hydraulic Weapon Carrier

Elmers Salvage Yard

Top;Eric Duellman in Part of
The Used Car Lot
Center; Elmer & Randy Arter-
burn Moving Cars for Pictures
Bottom Left; The Front Of One
Of Elmer's Racing Cars

Elmer's Junk Yard Dog
"CUJO"

Mid 1950's to Early 1960's
The Harvieux Family
Burnsville, MN

Kimball Sterling
Johnson City, TN

45 Mustang - 41 Chrysler
Allen Wilson
Amanda & Jason Wilson
Kingsville, TX

Mid 1960's Vehicles
Daniel & Kathy Rocha
Omaha, NE

Late 1950's Vehicles
Don Klang
Tacoma, WA

Fleet of Custom Built Pedal Cars
Dick King
Kelso, WA

The Harvieux Family
Burnsville,MN

Display at Local Museum
Nate & Charlene Stoller's Collection
Ripon,CA

Used Car Lot
Timothy Davis
Dallas,TX

Duffy's Collectible Cars
Cedar Rapids,IA

Dennis Dickson
Lebanon,OR

Dennis Dickson
Lebanon,OR

**Daniel & Kathy Rocha's Living & Dining Room (9-Pedal Cars, 1-Wagon, 1-Tricycle)
Omaha, NE**

**Daniel Rocha at a Flea Market in Saudi Arabia with Piles & Piles Of Pedal Cars and Parts
Photograph by Vito Spadaro
Omaha, NE**

**Daniel Rocha in His Front Yard with Part of His Collection
Omaha, NE**

1949 Garton
Tyler Hart-Grandson
Bud Swink
Morganton,NC

1939 Garton Ford "Woodie" with Trailer
Wayne Mitchell
Keller,TX

1925 American National
Wayne Mitchell
Keller,TX

1965 Ford Mustang
Robert Lambrecht
Billings,MT

1962 AMF Coca-Cola Delivery Truck
John Stegeman
Allegan,MI

1960's AMF Pepsi-Cola Delivery Truck
John Stegeman
Allegan,MI

1961 Murray Circus Car
John Stegeman
Allegan,MI

1962 AMF Dr.Pepper Delivery Truck
John Stegeman
Allegan,MI

1953 BMC
Driver-Brett Hart
William Swink
Morganton,NC

Murray SS T-Bird
Restored by Lineback & Sons
M.K.Lineback
Greensboro,NC

Murray T-Bird
Driver Brett Hart Grandson
Bud Swink
Morganton,NC

Restored 1926 Steelcraft Mack
Howdy Doody, Mickey, & Minnie Mouse In Car
Ross Steele
Madisonville,TN

Mr. Peanut by Kingsbury Toys
Robert Lambrecht
Billings,MT

1968 AMF Dr.Pepper Promotional Car
Brand New with Original Box
Greg & Karyl Donahue
Floral City,FL

1961 Murray Original
Greg Katason
Denver,CO

1950's Murray
Denny Spadone
Denville,NJ

1955 Murray Good Humor Truck
John Stegeman
Allegan,MI

1961 Murray 3-Wheeler
Richard H. Pate
Biddeford,ME

1950's Murray
John McKenzie
Seal Beach,FL

1955 Murray Dump Truck
Mike Paone
Berkeley Heights,NJ

1929 Steelcraft Mack Truck
Mr. & Mrs. Robert Lampman
Vernon,NY

1952 Garton Chaindrive Dumptruck #K752
Driver Kendra Vondrasek
Merle J. Vondrasek
Desoto,TX

1929 Steelcraft Mack Dump Truck
Driver Maddie Gottenborg
Restored & Owned By Phil Gottenborg
Galesburg,IL

1948 Murray Dump Truck
Don Klang
Tacoma,WA 98404

Early 1950's BMC Dumptruck
Restored by Dave Laduca
Lewiston,NY

1949 Pontiac Station Wagon-Driver Brandon Howes
Restored by Portell Restorations
Paul & Linda Accarpio
Manchester,CT

1949 Pontiac Station Wagon
Allen Wilson
Kingsville,TX

1948 Murray Station Wagon
Danny Kent
Eaton Park,FL

1955 Murray Station Wagon #741
Driver Robert Paone
Mike Paone
Berkeley Heights, NJ

1955 Murray Station Wagon
Driver Einstein
Daniel & Kathy Rocha
Omaha,NE

1958 Murray Champion Station Wagon
Driver Einstein
Daniel & Kathy Rocha
Omaha,NE

Restored 1949 Murray Station Wagon #F 641
Timothy Davis
Dallas,TX

1949 Garton Station Wagon
Steve Castelli
Windsor,CA

1963 Murray Deluxe Station Wagon #W-751
Richard Bio
Providence,RI

1930's Garton V8 Station Wagon
K.David Brown
St. Augustine,FL

1948 Murray Station Wagon
Rodney Breeze
Lawton,OK

1955 Murray Station Wagon
Rodney Breeze
Lawton,OK

1949 Garton Air Force Jeep
Robert Lambrecht
Billings,MT

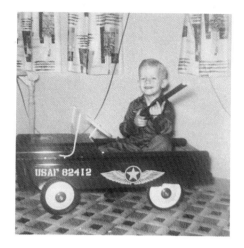

1961 Garton Air Force Jeep #5640
Richard Davis 4 Years Old
Richard Davis
Garland,TX

1959 Garton U.S. Army Jeep #5622
Kendra Vondrasek Driver
Merle J. Vondrasek
Desoto,Tx

1960 Hamilton Air Force Jeep
Restored by Bygone Toys
Frank & Irlene Gordon
Leawood,KS

1991 Jungle Safari Jeep
Laurie Haver
Williamsville,NY

1950's AMF Jeep
Don Knox
Oshkosh,WI

1950 Caterpillars
Doc Hunkler
Russiaville,IN

1957 Farmall 560
John Reinhardt
Florissant,MO

1950's Jeep & Murray Tractor
Steve Castelli
Windsor,CA

1958 AMF Steger
Bud Swink
Morganton,NC

1955 AMF U.S.Mail Truck
Driver David Pickering
Ron Pickering
Ft. Lauderdale,FL

(Before)
1950's AMF D-4 Cat Bulldozer
Premer Motors
Evans,CO

(After)
1950's AMF D-4 Cat Bulldozer
Restored by Premer Motors
Evans,CO

Castelli Tractor Original
Castelli Co. Out of Philadelphia
Steve Castelli
Windsor,CA

1955 John Deere Tractor
Robert Lambrecht
Billings,MT

1960 D-60 Tractor
Restored by Bygone Toys
Frank & Irlene Gordon
Leawood,KS

Daughter Jamie with Trophy
1st Place Tractor Pulls
Mike Elwell
Cottage Grove,MN

Mike Jr. with Trophy
3rd Place in Tractor Pulls
Mike Elwell
Cottage Grove,MN

Son Jeff on Pedal Construction Toy
Mike Elwell
Cottage Grove,MN

1950's AMF Bulldozer Original
Steve Castelli
Windsor,CA

Murray Boat with Motor
Allen Wilson
Kingsville,Tx

1960's Murray Boat-Custom Painted
Restored by Lineback & Sons
M.K.Lineback
Greensboro,NC

Murray Boat #9-960
Merle J. Vondrasek
Desoto,TX

Restored 1967 Murray Skipper Run-A-Bout
Model #8-961
Timothy Davis
Dallas,TX

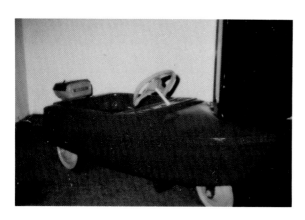

1958 Murray Boat
Fred Forster
West Milford,NJ

Restored Murray Boat with After Market Motor
Richard Pate
Biddeford,ME

(Before)
1960's Murray Super Sonic Jet
Premer Motors
Evans,CO

(After)
1960's Murray Super Sonic Jet
Restored by Premer Motors
Evans,CO

Steelcraft Air Ace
Steve Castelli
Windsor,CA

Early 1920's Artic Byrd
Pilot Charlie McCarthy
Ross Steele
MadisonVille,TN

1940's Murray Pursuit Plane
Restored by Bygone Toys-1989 Kalamazoo Winner
Frank & Irlene Gordon
Leawood,KS

1945 Murray "Flying Tiger"
Restored by Bygone Toys
Frank Gordon
Leawood,KS

1961 Murray Atomic Missile
Jerome Schaut
St.Marys,PA

1941 Steelcraft Spitfire
Restored by Portell Restorations
Dan Portell
Hematite,MO

1935 Keystone Ride On Plane
Stan Phillips
Oakmont,PA

1941 Pursuit Plane-Driver Maddie Gottenborg
Restored Into Gee-Bee Racer By Phil Gottenborg
Phil Gottenborg
Galesburg,IL

Restored 1946 Murray Pursuit Plane
Richard H. Pate
Biddeford,ME

1940 Murray Navy Pursuit Plane
Fred Forster
West Milford,NJ

Restored 1941 Steelcraft U.S. Pursuit Plane #B695
Timothy Davis
Dallas,TX

1945 Murray U.S. Pursuit Plane
Rodney Breeze
Lawton,OK

1941 Murray Pursuit Plane
Bud & Betty's Garndson
Mr. & Mrs. Lampman
Vernon,NY

1955 Murray Sky Streak
Greg & Karyl Donahue
Floral City,FL

1946 Pursuit Plane"Flying Tiger"
Richard Pate
Biddeford,ME

Built by William Wiggins
William Wiggins
Tacoma,WA

1950 Murray
Bob Ellsworth
Taylors,SC

1960's Murray Pedal Rocket
Owned by Lineback & Sons
Greensboro,NC

1933 American National Lincoln
Owner Jack Davidson,Fresno,CA
Picture Taken by Alex Dalmatoff
Fresno,CA

1990's Woodie Built by K.David Brown
Used 2 1960's AMF Cars-Over 5 1/2 Feet Long
David & Erica Brown-K.David's Gallery
St.Augustine,FL

1933 Gendron Lincoln
Sold at Kerry Holders Collecters Auction
Springfield,MO

1934 Steelcraft Tandem
Pat Guiney
Nashue,NH

1934 American National Tandem
Mike Paone
Berkley Heights,NJ

1934 American National Tandem
Restored by Portell Restorations
Auto Carousel-Portell Restorations
Hematite.MO

1948 Murray
Steve Castelli
Windsor,CA

AMF Hook & Ladder
Jim Parkhurst
Bridgeton,NJ

1941 Steelcraft Buick Fire Chief Car
Restored by Portell Restorations
Dan Portell
Hematite,MO

Early 1970's AMF Fire Chief
Richard Bio
Providence,RI

1970's AMF Sears Fire Fighter
Richard Bio
Providence,RI

1959 Murry Fire Truck
Dennis Dickson
Lebanon,OR

1948 Murray Fire Truck
Restored by Bygone Toys
Frank & Irlene Gordon
Leawood,KS

1949 Pontiac Fire Truck
Original Body & Paint-Driver Bryan Howes
Paul & Linda Accarpio
Manchester,CT

1959 Murray Fire Engine
Fred Forster
West Milford,NJ

Late 1970's AMF Fire Fighter
Richard Bio
Providence,RI

1934 American National Fire Truck
Restored by Portell Restorations
Dan Portell
Hematite,MO

1963 AMF Fire Chief #503 Original
Grandaughter-Kendra Vondrasek
Merle J. Vondrasek
Desoto,TX

Restored 1948 Murray Fire Engine
This Car Was on a Carnival Ride
Nate & Charlene Stoller Collection

1953 BMC Hook & Ladder
Robert Paone Driver
Mike Paone
Berkeley Heights,NJ

1950 Murray 506 Fire Chief Car
Restored by Portell Restorations
Hematite,MO

1934 American National Fire Truck
Kerry Holder
Springfield,MO

1960 AMF Fire Chief
Harold & Judy Arrington
Wichita Falls,TX

Early 1930's Steelcraft 2 1/2 Ton Bull Dog Mack
All Original
Connie Stanley
Vidor,TX

Restored 1955 Murray Fire Engine
Nate & Charlene Stoller Collection
Ripon,CA

1935 Air Flow Chrysler Fire Truck Steelcraft
Dick Traugh
Giants Pass,OR

Early Pedal / Pull Car
John Stegeman
Allegan,MI

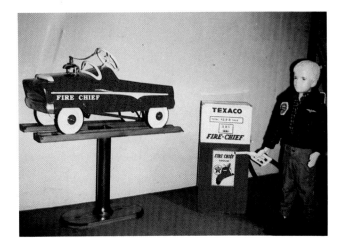

1962 Garton
John Stegeman
Allegan,MI

1941 Steelcraft Buick
Charlie McCarthy in Car
Ross Steele
Madisonville,TN

1948 Murray Fire Truck
Dave Laduca
Lewiston.NY

(Before) 1924 American National Fire Truck
Owned by John Borgna
Restored by Doc Hunkler
Russiaville, IN

(After) 1924 American National Fire Truck
Owned by Jon Borgna
Restored by Doc Hunkler
Russiaville, IN

1941 Murray Dodge
Doc Hunkler
Russiaville, IN

1938 Garton Pontiac
Restored by Doc Hunkler
Russiaville, IN

1925 American National
Doc Hunkler
Russiaville, IN

1937 Steelcraft Airflow
Owned by Ken Lusk
Restored by Doc Hunkler
Russiaville, IN

1968 Murray Firetruck
John Stegeman
Allegan,MI

1968 Murray Firetruck
John Stegeman
Allegan,MI

1968 Murray Firetruck
John Stegeman
Allegan,MI

Shane & Justin In Car Lot
William Severeid
Mishawaka,IN

1955 Murray
Driver-Justin
William Severeid
Mishawaka,IN

1968 Boat
Betty Klang
Tacoma,WA

1934 Boycraft Fire Truck
Lauruen Singleton in Picture
Randy Arterburn
Indianapolis,IN

1929 Steelcrfat Dump Truck
Randy Arterbun
Indianapolis,IN

1925 Gendron Dump Truck
Randy Arterburn
Indianapolis,IN

1941 Steelcraft Fire Truck
Randy Arterburn
Indianapolis,IN

1949 Garton Fire Truck
Randy Arterburn
Indianapolis,IN

1959 Garton
Driver Tyler Hart-Grandson
William Swink
Morganton,NC

MG Model M6-TD Molded Plastic
Made In Brazil by Baneirante
Blaine Linkous
Fallston,MD

MG Model M6-TD Made In England
Battery Operated Headlights
Blaine Linkous
Fallston,MD

1941 Chrysler Steelcraft
Duffy's Collectible Cars
Cedor Rapids,IA

1921 American All Original
Lonnie Stanley
Vidor,TX

Restored 1948 Murray Comet
Nate & Charlene Stoller Collection
Ripon,CA

1965 AMF Mustang
Roseana Sims
Cedar Hill,TX

207

1990's Racioppo & Scala Vehicle
Racioppo & Scala Pedal Vehicles
New Castle,PA

1990's Racioppo & Scala Vehicle
Racioppo & Scala Pedal Vehicles
New Castle,PA

1960 Murray T-Bird
A Valentines Gift
Veronica Doster
Athens,GA

1953 Torpedo
Veronica Doster
Athens,GA

AMF Pacer
Veronica Doster
Athens,GA

1930's Skippy
Veronica Doster
Athens,GA

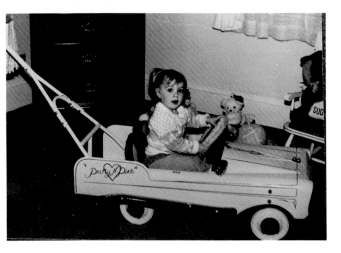

Late 1970's AMF(Fire Fighter)
Richard Bio
Providence,RI

1980's Smurf Mobile-Plastic Mfg. Unknown
Driver Alexandria Nicole Bio
Richard Bio
Providence,RI

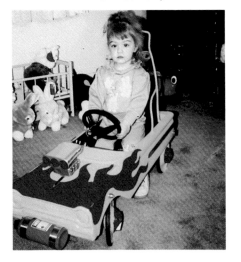

1970 AMF Fire Chief-Custom Made
Driver Alexandria Nicole Bio
Richard Bio
Providence,RI

1937 Garton Pontaic
Alex Dalmatoff
Fresno,CA

1941 Chrysler Steelcraft
Driver Jessica
Alex Dalmatoff
Fresno,CA

Alex Dalmatoff's Business Card
Pedal To The Metal
Fresno,CA

1955 Champion-Restored by Portell Restorations
Driver Brandon Howes-Greatnephew
Paul & Linda Accarpio
Manchester,CT

1949 Comet-Restored by Portell Restorations
Driver Bryan Howes-Greatnephew
Paul & Linda Accarpio
Manchester,CT

1969 Mustang Original Body & Paint
Driver Bryan Howes-Greatnephew
Paul & Linda Accarpio
Manchester,CT

Restored 1935 Steelcraft Pontiac
Driver Bryan Howes-Greatnephew
Paul & Linda Accarpio
Manchester,Ct

1960, 1948, 1955 Murray's & Car Hauling Trailor
Dean Applegate
Warren,OH

1950 Murray
K.L.Jestes
Boca Raton,FL

**Restored 1930 Gendron Packard
Restored by Portell Restorations
Dan Portell
Hematite,MO**

**1934 Steelcraft
Restored by Portell Restorations
Dan Portell
Hematite,MO**

**1939 Steelcraft Lincoln
Restored by Portell Restorations
Dan Portell
Hematite,MO**

**1927 Garton Kissil
Restored by Preston Williams
Dan Portell
Hematite,MO**

**1961 Murray Teebird
Total Authentic Restoration
Greg Donahue
Floral City,FL**

**1941 Chrysler Steelcraft
Rodney Breeze
Lawton,OK**

1961 Garton
Timothy J. Davis
Dallas,TX

1926 Gendron Dodge
Timothy J. Davis
Dallas,TX

1990 Hand Made Original
Roberta Brown
Redland,CA

1949 Murray Buick
John Cristando
Elmont,NY

1930 Boycraft Cadillac
Driver 1917 Doll
Mr. & Mrs. Bob Colligan
Loudonville,NY

1941 Chrysler & 1936 Air Flow
Sandhill Antiques
Ralph Stimson,Larry Cirkl
Robins,IA

1953 Garton
John Stegeman
Allegan,MI

1962 Murray Maverick
John Stegeman
Allegan,MI

1961 Murray "Gilmore Speedway"
John Stegeman
Allegan,MI

1961 Murray TeeBird
John Stegeman
Allegan,MI

1962 Murray Station Wagon
John Stegeman
Allegan,MI

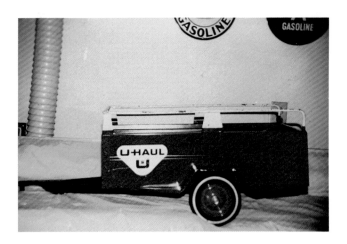

U-Haul Original
Dennis Dickson
Lebanon, OR

1965 Murray
Dennis Dickson
Lebanon, OR

1960's Murray
Dennis Dickson
Lebanon, OR

Restored 1955 Murray
Dennis Dickson
Lebanon, OR

Early 1950's Murray
Dennis Dickson
Lebanon, OR

1940's Garton Original
Dennis Dickson
Lebanon, OR

1960 AMF
Betty Klang
Tacoma,WA

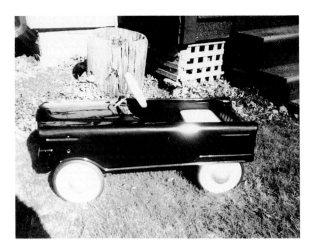

Late 1950's murray
Betty Klang
Tacoma,WA

1950's BMC
Don Klang
Tacoma,WA

1960's Murray
Bob Ellsworth
Taylors,SC

1960 Murray
Bob Ellsworth
Taylors,SC

1968 AMF Police Car with Working Red Light Siren
Formerly 503 Fire Chief
Danny R. Fisher
Garland,TX

1950 Garton Racer
Mike Elwell
Cottage Grove,MN

1937 Steelcraft Buick
Dan Fitzgerald
Thornton,CO

1934 Chrysler Steelcraft
Dan Fitzgerald
Thornton,CO

1950's AMF
Driver Ashley Davis
Richard Davis
Garland,TX

1970's AMF
Thomas Davis
Garland,TX

1960's AMF Doing a Little Advertising
For Partin's Paint & Body Shop
Photo by K.David Brown
St.Augustine,FL

1941 Chrsler Steelcraft
Sandhill Antiques
Robins,IA

1952 Murray Champion
Restored by Kevin Bennett
Ownwer Don Mayfield, Kevin Bennett
Zillah,WA

1939 Steelcraft Supercharger(Before)
Kevin Bennett
Zillah,WA

Restored 1939 Steelcraft Supercharger(After)
Owner Del Matthews
Kevin Bennett
Zillah,WA

Teens Racer
Kevin Bennett
Zillah,WA

1966 AMF Jetsweep
Owner & Driver Philip Bennett
Kevin Bennett
Zillah,WA

Trike with Side Car
Harriet Fork
Gibsonburg,OH

1925 Gendron
Jay Glerum
New Oxford,PA

1935 Steelcraft
Don Knox
Oshkosh,WI

1924 Toledo
Don Knox
Oshkosh,WI

1960's Murray
The Harvieux Family
Burnsville,MN

1961 Garton
David Huffhines
Garland,TX

1959-60's Gyn Vanoy Surrey
Memory Lane Classics
Perrysburg,OH

1990's Hand Made Pedal Vehicles
King Kraft-Dick King
Kelso,WA

1990 Sedan Delivery with 1960's Style Wood Boat
King Kraft-Dick King
Kelso,WA

1990 Pro-Sidewalk
King Kraft-Dick King
Kelso,WA

1990 Flatbed
King Kraft-Dick King
Kelso,WA

1990 Gas Truck
King Kraft-Dick King
Kelso,WA

1965 AMF Mustang
George Haver
Williamsville,NY

1965 AMF Mustang
Restored by Dave Luduca
Laurie Haver
Williamsville,NY

1941 Murray Chrysler
Restored by Bygone Toys
Frank & Irlene Gordon
Leawood,KS

1950 Garton Kidillac
Restored by Bygone Toys
Frank & Irlene Gordon
Leawood,KS

1941 Chrysler Murray-"2 of a Kind"
Restored by Bygone Toys
Frank & Irlene Gordon
Leawood,KS

1936 Steelcraft Chrysler Airflow
Restored by Bygone Toys
Frank & Irlene Gordon
Leawood,KS

1930's Steelcraft Skippy
Mr. & Mrs. Robert Lampman
Vernon,NY

1928 Packard
Mr. & Mrs. Robert Lampman
Vernon,NY

1932 Steelcraft Ford
Mr. & Mrs. Robert Lampman
Vernon,NY

1960's AMF Command Car
Robert Lambrecht
Billings,MT

1960's Stutz-Bear-Cat by Marx
Robert Lambrecht
Billings,MT

1940's Garton
Robert Lambrecht
Billings,MT

1937 Steelcraft Chevy
Restored by Phil Gottenborg
Phil Gottenborg
Galesburg, IL

1941 Steelcraft Chrysler
Restored by Phil Gottenborg
Phil Gottenborg
Galesburg, IL

Restored 1930 Steelcraft Chrysler
Driver Maddie Gottenborg
Phil Gottenborg
Galesburg, IL

1926 Chevy
Larry Farnham
Minneapolis, MN

1934 "Motor"-Bike (Before)
Larry Farnham
Minneapolis, MN

1934 "Motor"-Bike (After)
Larry Farnham
Minneapolis, MN

1950's Garton
Driver Molly Ricci-4th Birthday
Danny Kent
Eaton Park,FL

1910 Hudson
Kerry Holder
Springfield,MO

1918 Gendron
Kerry Holder
Springfield,MO

Pedal Car Sold At Kerry Holder's Auction
Kerry Holder
Springfield,MO

1910 Car Unknown
Kerry Holder
Springfield,MO

1915 Pacard
Kerry Holder
Springfield,MO

1953 Murray Champion Model L-610
Restored by Dave Laduca
David Laduca
Lewiston,NY

1961 Murray Fire Chief & 1961 Murray Teebird
Dave Luduca
Lewiston,NY

Early 1950's Steelcraft/BMC Thunderbolt
David Luduca
Lewiston,NY

1950 Triang(England)
Goodguys
Gary Meadors
Alamo,CA

1934 Steelcraft
Pat Guiney
Nashua,NH

1936 Steelcraft
Sold At Kimball Sterling Auction
Jonesboro,TN

1941 Steelcraft Chrysler
John McKenzie
Seal Beach, CA

1923 Jitney by Toledo
Stan Phillips
Oakmont, PA

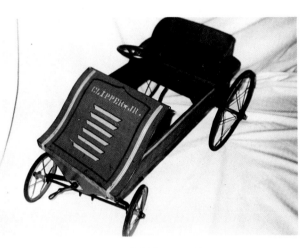

1915 Clipper Jr.
Stan Phillips
Oakmont, PA

1948 Murray Torpedo
Richard H. Pate
Biddeford, ME

Late 1930's Steelcraft Chrysler Airflow
Was Originally Fire Truck
Richard H. Pate
Biddeford, ME

1949 Murray
Richard H. Pate
Biddeford, ME

Late 1920's-Early 1930's Steelcraft
Pat Guiney
Nashua,NH

1961 Murray Happytime Sportster
Laurie Haver
Williamsville,NY

1990 Car
Built by Bill Wiggins
William Wiggins
Tacoma,WA

1990 Car
Built by Bill Wiggins
William Wiggins
Tacoma,WA

1950's Triang Racer (English)
Driver Matthew
Maynard Smith
Scranton,KS

1950's Murray Champion Customized
Driver Matthew-Grandson
Maynard Smith
Scranton,KS

1950's Murray Torpedo
Daniel & Kathy Rocha
Omaha,NE

1965 AMF Mustang
Daniel & Kathy Rocha
Omaha,NE

1958 Murray Champion
Driver Einstein
Daniel & Kathy Rocha
Omaha,NE

Russian Pedal Car Bought in Athens on the Way
Home From Desert Storm-Driver Einstein
Daniel & Kathy Rocha
Omaha,NE

Saudi Arabian in a Pedal Truck
Photo by Daniel Rocha in Saudi Arabia
Daniel & Kathy Rocha
Omaha,NE

Restored 1950's Garton
Nate & Charlene Stoller Collection
Ripon,CA

1959 Murray Ford
Restored by Lineback & Sons
M.K.Lineback
Greensboro,NC

1948 Pontiac
Restored by Lineback & Sons
M.K.Lineback
Greensboro,NC

1940's Garton
Restored by Lineback & Sons
M.K.Lineback
Greensboro,NC

1916 Gendron
Raggedy Ann in Car
Ross Steele
Madisonville,TN

1986 #1 Wood Pedal Car
Built by Ross Steele-Howdy Doody in Car
Ross Steele
Madisonville,TN

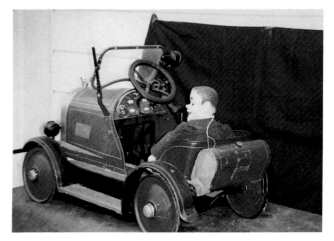

1921 American National Oldsmobile
Charlie McCarthy in Car
Ross Steele
Madisonville,TN

1953 Murray Champion with U-Haul Trailor

1929 Steelcraft Auburn
Driver-Grandson Jimmy
Gene Kirsch
Roseville,MN

1927 American National Lincoln Speedster
Gene Kirsch
Roseville,MN

Todd Block's Fleet of Cars
St.Peter,MN

1961 Murray & U-Haul
Bill Swaney
Mars, PA

1955 Kidillac
Gold Plating
Bill Swaney
Mars, PA

1953 Murray Sad Face
Bill Swaney
Mars, PA

1958 BMC Thunderbolt
Bill Swaney
Mars, PA

1965 Mustang
Bill Swaney
Mars, PA

1957 Midwest Industries-Jet Hawk
Bill Swaney
Mars, PA

Restored 1958 Murray Champion
Nate & Charlene Stoller Collection
Ripon,CA

Restored 1960's 501 AMF Jet-sweep
Nate & Charlene Stoller Collection
Ripon,CA

Restored 1948 Murray Comet
Nate & Charlene Stoller Collection
Ripon,CA

1934 Skippy Airflow Desoto Roadster
Dick Traugh
Grants Pass,OR

1935 Steelcraft Airflow Chrysler Roadster
Dick Traugh
Grants Pass,OR

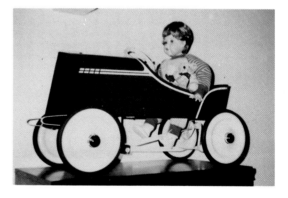

1933 Garton Sport Roadster
Merle J. Vondrasek
Desoto,TX

1925 Packard Roadster
Herman Zalvd
North Platte,NE

Early 1920's
Herman Zalvd
North Platte,NE

1925 Pierce Arrow
Herman Zalvd
North Platte,NE

1941 Steelcraft Chrysler
Jerry Turk
Edgewater,MD

1955 Murray
Jerry Turk
Edgewater,MD

1950's AMF
Bud Swink
Morgaton,NC

1961 Jet-Sweep Original
John Reinhardt
Florissant,MO

1960's Murray Fire Ball Racer
John Stegeman
Allegan,MI

1953 BMC Thunderbolt
John Stegeman
Allegan,MI

1958 Murray
John Stegeman
Allegan,MI

1962 Garton Mark V
John Stegeman
Allegan,MI

1960's AMF Ford Falcon
Restored by Lineback & Sons
M.K.Lineback
Greensboro,NC

1950 Murray Champion-Custom Painted
Restored by Lineback & Sons
M.K.Lineback
Greensboro,NC

1940's Garton "Casey Jones"
Drivers Jessica & Dustin Lineback
M.K.Lineback
Greensboro,NC

1949 Murray Buick
M.K.Lineback
Greensboro,NC

1949 BMC Thunderbolt
M.K.Lineback
Greensboro,NC

1960's AMF Ford Falcon
Restored by Lineback & Sons
M.K.Lineback
Greensboro,NC

1935 Skippy Desoto
Restored by Premer Motors
Evans,CO

1960's AMF Original
Jim Parkhurst
Bridgeton,NJ

1935 Toledo Studebaker
Driver Robert Paone
Mike Paone
Berkeley Heights,NJ

1940 Gendron Skippy
Driver Robert Paone
Mike Paone
Berkeley Heights,NJ

Restored 1932 Cadillac
Jan Mowery
Lincoln,NE

Restored Early 1960's Murray T-Bird
Daniel Morrow
Fleming,OH

1958 Murray
Robert Vos & Associates
Coral Springs,FL

1960's Murray
Bob Ellsworth
Taylors,SC

1960's Murray
Bob Ellsworth
Taylors,SC

1948 Garton
Steve Castelli
Windsor,CA

This Page Are All Merle J. Vondrasek's Cars With His Grandaughter Kendra as the Driver

1959 Murray Ford Custom
Desoto,TX

1965 AMF Mustang Sport Deluxe
Desoto,TX

1927 UHLEN #65
Desoto,TX

1937 Garton Packard #5711
Desoto,TX

1949 Murray Torpedo Deluxe
Desoto,TX

1961 Murray Teebird Custom Paint
Desoto,TX

1941 Steelcraft Pontaic
Desoto,TX

1939 Steelcraft Lincoln Zephyr
Desoto,TX

237

1937 Steelcraft
The Harvieux Family
Burnsville,MN

1938 Adler-Sport
Fritz Erckens
Krämerstrabe 23,Deutachland

1933 London Buick
100% Original Condition
Fritz Erckens
Krämerstrabe 23,Deutachland

1938 Steelcraft Pontiac
Bob & Pamela Colligan
Loudonville,NY

1909 Hales Flyer
Steve Castelli
Windsor,CA

1910 Keystone
Steve Castelli
Windsor,CA

1948 Murray Buick
Steve Castelli
Windsor,CA

1928 Steelcraft Buick
Steve Castelli
Windsor,CA

1928 Steelcraft Hudson
Steve Castelli
Windsor,CA

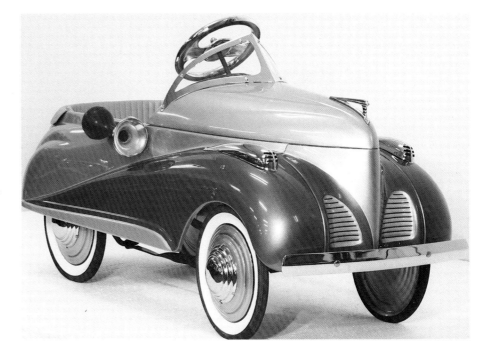

1939 Lincoln Zephyr
Restored by Premer Motors
Premer Motors
Evans,CO

1906 American
Premer Motors
Paul & Naomi Premer
Evans,CO

Restored D-4 Cat Bulldozer &
Restored Super Sonic Jet
Drivers Mark & Mindy Larum
Premer Motors-Paul & Naomi
Evans,CO

(Before)
1941 Steelcraft Streamliner
Premer Motors
Paul & Naomi Premer
Evans,CO

(After)
1941 Steelcraft Streamliner
Restored by Premer Motors
Paul & Naomi Premer
Evans,CO

1928 Packard
Paul & Naomi Premer
Evans,CO

1952 Garton Tin Lizzie
Jake The Guard Dog
Tom Vitunic
Allison Park,PA

1958 Murray Deluxe Champion
Tom Vitunic
Allison Park,PA

1968 AMF Super Sport
With Luggage Rack
Tom Vitunic
Allison Park,PA

1941 Steelcraft Chrysler
Tom Vitunic
Allison Park,PA

Tom Vitunics Used Car Lot
Allison Park,PA

Aaron & Matthew Niverson
Sons of Ed & Beth Niverson
Ed Is Shipping Engineer At
L-W Book Sales

1933 Lincoln American
National
Driver-Sean Hooley
Car From the Frank Hooley
Collection
Troy,NY

1960's Boat with Motor &
1960's Murray's Super-
Sonic Jet
Steve Castelli
Windsor,CA

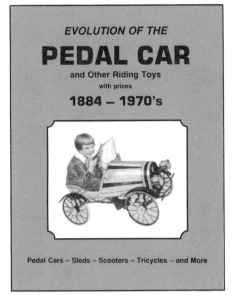
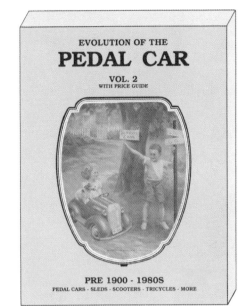
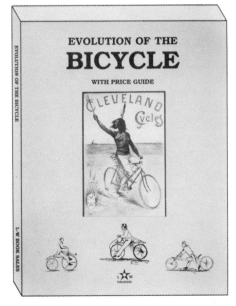

Price Guide

The price guide in this book is for Pedal Cars in good to excellent condition. Cars found with parts missing, very poor paint, wheels changed from originals, or excessive rust will bring much lower prices. A car considered to be in good condition is one with original paint and no parts missing. A car in excellent condition is one that is 70% to 95% mint. This price guide is based on cars in these conditions. L-W BOOKS can not be responsible for gains or losses as this is only a guide.

All Prices Are Of Pedal Cars Unless Otherwise Specified

PAGE 17
Top - $600+
Bottom - $800+
PAGE 18
Top - $700+
Bottom - $700+
PAGE 19
Top - $1400+
Bottom - $750+
PAGE 20
Top - $1800+
Middle - $4000+
Bottom - $1600+
PAGE 21
Top - $1400+
Middle - $3700+
Bottom - $900+
PAGE 22
Top - $1800+
Middle - $3500+
Bottom - $2200+
PAGE 23
Top - $250+
Middle - $200+
Bottom - $600+
PAGE 24
Top Left - $4000+
Top Right - $35000+
Bottom - $9000+
PAGE 25
Top - $3000+
Bottom - $3000+
PAGE 26
Top - $9000+
PAGE 27
Top - $8000+

PAGE 28
Top - $4500+
Bottom Left - $4000+
Bottom Right - $4000+
PAGE 29
Top - $9000+
PAGE 30
Top - $3500+
Bottom - $3200+
PAGE 31
Top - $3200+
Bottom - $3500+
PAGE 32
Top - $5000+
PAGE 33
Top - $3500+
Bottom - $3500+
PAGE 34
Top - $3000+
Bottom - $3500+
PAGE 35
Top - $4500+
Bottom - same
PAGE 36
Top - $3200+
PAGE 37
Top - $2000+
Bottom Left - $1400+
Bottom Right - $1400+
PAGE 38
Top - $3200+
Bottom - $3000+
PAGE 39
Top - $1400+
Bottom - $1500+
PAGE 40

PAGE 41
Top - $4000+
Bottom - $4000+
PAGE 41
Top - $7000+
Bottom - $9000+
PAGE 42
Reference only
PAGE 43
Top - $2600+
Bottom - $3000+
PAGE 44
Top - $3400+
Bottom - $3400+
PAGE 45
Top - $20000+
Bottom - $18000+
PAGE 46
Top - $3000+
Bottom - $3200+
PAGE 47
Top - $5000+
Bottom - $12000+
PAGE 48
Top - $3000+
Bottom - $4000+
PAGE 49
Top - $7000+
Bottom - $15000+
PAGE 50
Top - $4000+
Bottom - $4000+
PAGE 51
Top - $900+
Middle - $950+
Bottom - $1000+
PAGE 52

PAGE 52
Top - $3400+
Bottom -$3500+
PAGE 53
Top - $1600+
Bottom - $2000+
PAGE 54
Top - $3500+
Bottom - $3500+
PAGE 55
Top - $3500+
Bottom - $3700+
PAGE 56
Top - $6000+
Bottom - $8000+
PAGE 57
Top - $3200+
Bottom - $3500+
PAGE 58
Top - $3500+
Bottom -$3500+
PAGE 59
Top - $4000+
Bottom - $6000+
PAGE 60
Top - $1100+
Bottom - $1400+
PAGE 61
Top - $1400+
Bottom - $3200+
PAGE 62
Top - $2000+
Bottom - $2000+
PAGE 63
Reference only
PAGE 64
Top - $14000+

Bottom - $25000+

PAGE 65

Top - $1800+

Bottom - $3000+

PAGE 66

Top - $1500+

Bottom - $900+

PAGE 67

Top - $2000+

Bottom -Reference only

PAGE 68

Top - $3000+

Bottom - $3000+

PAGE 69

Top - $3000+

Bottom - $2200+

PAGE 70

Top - $2500+

Bottom - $16000+

PAGE 71

Top - $25000+

Bottom - $25000+

PAGE 72

Top - $4000+

Bottom - $6000+

PAGE 73

Top - $1200+

Middle - $1400+

Bottom - $1500+

PAGE 74

Top - $3500+

Bottom - $2200+

PAGE 75

Top - $1800+

Bottom - $2000+

PAGE 76

Top - $3400+

Bottom - $3600+

PAGE 77

Top - $3400+

Bottom - $3600+

PAGE 78

Top - $4000+

Bottom - $3500+

PAGE 79

Top - $3500+

Bottom - $4000+

PAGE 80

Top - $18000+

Bottom - $7000+

PAGE 81

Top - $4000+

Bottom - $7000+

PAGE 82

Top - $1200+

Bottom - $2500+

PAGE 83

Top - $4000+

Bottom - $7000+

PAGE 84

Top - $2500+

Bottom - $3200+

PAGE 85

Top - $1400+

Bottom - $1200+

PAGE 86

Top - $2000+

Bottom - $2200+

PAGE 87

Top - $900+

Middle - $1200+

Bottom - $900+

PAGE 88

Top - $3500+

Bottom - $4000+

PAGE 89

Top - $3500+

Bottom - $3500+

PAGE 90

Top - $2500+

Bottom - $2200+

PAGE 91

Top - $2200+

Bottom - $4500+

PAGE 92

Top - $3000+

Bottom - $3200+

PAGE 93

Top - $1100+

Middle - $1400+

Bottom - $2200+

PAGE 94

Top - $900+

Middle - $1000+

Bottom - $1000+

PAGE 95

Top - $3500+

Bottom - $9000+

PAGE 96

Top - $5000+

Bottom - $4000+

PAGE 97

Top - $3000+

Bottom - $7000+

PAGE 98

Top - $2500+

Bottom - $4500+

PAGE 99

Top - $1200+

Bottom - $1500+

PAGE 100

Top - $2000+

Bottom - $2500

PAGE 101

Top - $2200+

Bottom - $2800+

PAGE 102

Top - $900+

Bottom - $1200+

PAGE 103

Top - $2500+

Bottom - $2500+

PAGE 104

Top - $2500+

Bottom - $2800+

PAGE 105

Top - $2500+

Bottom - $2500+

PAGE 106

Top - $2500+

Bottom - $2500+

PAGE 107

Top - $3500+

PAGE 108

Top - $3000+

Bottom - $1800+

PAGE 109

Top - $1200+

Bottom - $1800+

PAGE 110

Top - $900+

Middle - $900+

Bottom - $1200+

PAGE 111

Top - $1800+

Bottom - $2000+

PAGE 112

Top - $2000+

Bottom - $2200+

PAGE 113

Top - $3000+

Bottom - $3000+

PAGE 114

Top - $900+

Middle -$900+

Bottom - $1500+

PAGE 115

Top - $4000+

Bottom - $3500+

PAGE 116

Top - $1400+

Bottom - $2500+

PAGE 117

Top - $900+

Middle - $900+

Bottom - $1200+

PAGE 118

Top - $1200+

Bottom - $2000+

PAGE 119

Top - $2000+

Bottom - $1200+

PAGE 120

Top - $1800+

Bottom - $2500+

PAGE 121

Top - $2000+

Bottom - $2500+

PAGE 122

Top - $2500+ each

PAGE 123

Top - $3000+

Bottom - $2500+

PAGE 124

Top - $1800+

Bottom - $2200+

PAGE 125

Top - $1800+

Bottom - $2000+

PAGE 126

Top - $800+

PAGE 127

Magazine Ads - $3-$5+

PAGE 128

Magazine Ads - $3-$5+

PAGE 129

Magazine Ads - $3-$5+

PAGE 130

Magazine Page - $3-$5+

PAGE 131

Calendar - $25+

PAGE 132

All Postcards -$20-$30+

Top Left - $1000+

Top Right - $200+

2nd Left - $800+

2nd Right - $1000+

3rd Left - $400+

3rd Right - Ref. Only

Bottom Left - $200+

Bottom Right - $3000+

PAGE 133

All Postcards -$20-$30+

Top Left - $1200+

Top Right - $1000+

2nd Left - $1000+

2nd Right - $1000+

3rd Left - $1200+

3rd Right - $1000+

Bottom Left - $2000+

Bottom Right - $1000+

PAGE 134

All Postcards -$20-$30+

Except-2nd ,3rd,&

Bottom Left - $10+

Top Left - $2000+
Top Right - $300+
2nd Left - $400+
2nd Right - $1000+
3rd Left - $150+
3rd Right - $1000+
Bottom Left - Unknown
Bottom Right - $600+

PAGE 135
All Postcards -$20-$30+
Top Left - $800+
Top Middle - $1200+
Top Right - $1000+
2nd Left - $2000+
2nd Middle - $1000+
2nd Right - $1000+
Bottom Left - $1500+
Bottom Middle -$1500+
Bottom Right - $1000+

PAGE 136
All Postcards -$20-$30+
Top Left - $1000+
Top Middle - $1000+
Top Right - $750+
2nd Left - $600+
2nd Middle - $200+
2nd Right - $300+
Bottom Left - $1000+
Bottom Middle -$800+
Bottom Right - $300+

PAGE 137
All Postcards -$20-$30+
Top Left - $800+
Top Middle - $600+
Top Right - $600+
2nd Left - $1000+
2nd Middle - $1500+
2nd Right - $200+
Bottom Left - $1000+
Bottom Middle -$600+
Bottom Right - $1000+

PAGE 138
All Postcards -$20-$30+
Top Left - $600+
Top Right - $1000+
2nd Left - $1000+
2nd Right - $1200+
3rd Left - $400+
3rd Right - $600+
Bottom Left - $1500+
Bottom Right - $1000+

PAGE 139
All Postcards -$20-$30+
Top Left - $500+
Top Right - $500+
2nd Left - $600+
2nd Right - $600+
3rd Left - $800+
3rd Right - Ref. Only

Bottom Left - $600+
Bottom Right - $700+

PAGE 140
All Postcards -$20-$30+
Top Left - $500+
Top Right - $150+
2nd Left - $500+
2nd Right - $500+
3rd Left - $4000+
3rd Right - Comic
Bottom - $1000+

PAGE 141
All Postcards -$20-$30+
Top Left - $200+
Top Right - $600+
2nd Left - Ref. Only
2nd Right - $300+
3rd Left - $600+
3rd Right - $900+
Bottom Left - $600+
Bottom Right - $800+

PAGE 142
All Postcards -$20-$30+
Top Left - Comic
Top Right - $1000+
2nd Left - $400+
2nd Right - $600+
Bottom - $4000+

PAGE 143
All Postcards -$20-$30+
Top - $1800+
Middle - $1000+
Bottom - $4000+

PAGE 144
Top - $3000+

PAGE 145
Top - $4000+
Middle - $500+
Bottom - $1500+

PAGE 146
Top Left - $800+
Top Right - $1600+
Bottom Left - $2500+
Bottom Right -$15000+

PAGE 147
Top - $1500+
Bottom - $8000+

PAGE 148
Top - $1000+
Bottom Left - $3000+
Bottom Right - $600+

PAGE 149
Top - $400+
Middle - $10000+
Bottom - $1500+

PAGE 150
Top - $350+
Bottom - $800+

PAGE 151
Top - $300+
Bottom - $800+

PAGE 152
Top Left - $3200+
Top Right - $2000+
Middle Right - $350+
Bottom Left - $600+
Bottom Right - $1800+

PAGE 153
Calendar - $25+
Magazine Covers - $10+

PAGE 154
Calendar - $35+

PAGE 155
Calendar - $75+

PAGE 156
Magazine Ad - $10+

PAGE 157
Reference Only

PAGE 158
Top Left - $2000+
Top Right - $200+
Middle Left - $200+
Middle Right - $200+
Bottom Left - $800+
Bottom Right - $6000+

PAGE 159
Top Left - $3500+
Top Right - $2000+
Middle Left - $9500+
Middle Right - $1000+
Bottom Left - $10000+
Bottom Right - $3200+

PAGE 160
Top Left - $2000+
Top Right - $2000+
Middle Left - $3000+
Middle Right - $2000+
Bottom Left - $2000+
Bottom Right - $2000+

PAGE 161
Top Left - $200+
Top Right - $9500+
Middle Left - $1000+
Middle Right - $1700+
Bottom Left - $9000+
Bottom Right - $1500+

PAGE 162
Top Left - $1800+
Top Right - $7500+
Middle Left - $6500+
Middle Right - $700+
Bottom Left - $600+
Bottom Right - $600+

PAGE 163
Top Left - $7000+

Top Right - $5500+
Middle Left - $2000+
Middle Right - $2000+
Bottom Left - $700+
Bottom Right - $1500+

PAGE 164
Top Left - $7000+Rare
Top Right - $400+
Middle Left - $800+
Middle Right - $900+
Bottom Left - $4000+
Bottom Right - $500+

PAGE 165
Top Left - $4500+
Top Right - $650+
Middle Left - $1200+
Middle Right - $800+
Bottom Left - $500+
Bottom Right - $3000+

PAGE 166
Top Left - $2500+
Top Right - $900+
Middle Left-$1200+each
Middle Right - $1000+
Bottom Left - $12000+
Bottom Right - $6000+

PAGE 167
Top Left - $500+
Top Right - $900+
Middle Left - $4000+
Middle Right - $6000+
Bottom Left - $2500+
Bottom Right - $200+

PAGE 168
Top - $4000+
Middle - $6000+
Bottom - $4500+

PAGE 169
Top - $4000+
Middle - $2000+
Bottom - $1000+

PAGE 170
Top - $750+
Middle - $4000+
Bottom - $10000+

PAGE 171
Top - $5500+
Middle - $25000+
Bottom - $600+

PAGE 172
Top - $3500+
Middle - $1500+
Bottom - $700+

PAGE 173
Top - $5000+
Middle - $500+
Bottom - $800+

PAGE 174
Top - $5000+
Middle - $4000+
Bottom - $6000+
PAGE 175
Top - $9000+
PAGE 176
Top - $200+
Middle Left - $1500+
Middle Right - $6000+
Bottom - $5000+
PAGE 177
Top - $3500+ $3000+
2nd - $2500+ each
3rd - $2000+ $3000+
Bottom - $600+ each
PAGE 178
Top Left - $2500+
Top Right - $9000+
Middle Left - $1000+
Middle Right - $4000+
Bottom - $800+
PAGE 179
Reference Only
PAGE 180
Reference Only
PAGE 181
Reference Only
PAGE 182
Reference Only
PAGE 183
Top - $900+
Middle Left - $2500+
Middle Right - $1200+
Bottom - $400+
PAGE 184
Top Left - $350+
Top Right - $350+
Middle Left - $500+
Middle Right - $400+
Bottom - $500+
PAGE 185
Top Left - $200+
Top Right - $200+
Middle Left - $4000+
Middle Right - $200+
Bottom - $800+
PAGE 186
Top Left - $350+
Top Right - $250+
Middle Left - $350+
Middle Right - $500+
Bottom - $300+
PAGE 187
Top Left - $600+
Top Right - $4000+
Middle Left - $1000+

Middle Right - $4000+
Bottom Left - $400+
Bottom Right - $300+
PAGE 188
Top Left - $900+
Top Right - $1125+
Middle Left - $600+
Middle Right - $600+
Bottom Left - $600+
Bottom Right - $400+
PAGE 189
Top Left - $600+
Top Right - $1200+
Middle Left - $200+
Middle Right - $1500+
Bottom Left - $600+
Bottom Right - $450+
PAGE 190
Top Left - $250+
Top Right - $250+
Middle Left - $300+
Middle Right - $250+
Bottom Left - $60+
Bottom Right - $200+
PAGE 191
Top Left - $2200+ each
Top Right - $150+
Middle Left - $250+each
Middle Right - $200+
Bottom - $700+
PAGE 192
Top - Reference Only
Middle - $2000+
Bottom - $500+
PAGE 193
Top Left - $150+
Top Right - $150+
Middle Left - $150+
Middle Right - $100+
Bottom Left - $150+
Bottom Right - $2000+
PAGE 194
Top Left - $900+
Top Right - $200+
Middle Left - $500+
Middle Right - $700+
Bottom Left - $600+
Bottom Right - $800+
PAGE 195
Top - Reference Only
Middle - $800+
Bottom - $2000+
PAGE 196
Top Left - $3000+
Top Right - $2000+
Middle Left - $2200+
Middle Right - $500+
Bottom Left - $2000+

Bottom Right - $400+
PAGE 197
Top Left - $2000+
Top Right - $2000+
Middle Left - $2000+
Middle Right - $2000+
Bottom Left - $1500+
Bottom Right - $1500+
PAGE 198
Top Left - $400+
Top Right - $2200+
Middle Left - Contemporary
Middle Right - $2500+
Bottom Left - $2500+
Bottom Right - $300+
PAGE 199
Top Left - $12000+
Top Right - Contemporary
Middle Left - $2000+
Middle Right - $11500+
Bottom Left - $17000+
Bottom Right -$11000+
PAGE 200
Top Left - $600+
Top Right - $200+
Middle Left - $4000+
Middle Right-$150each
Bottom Left - $150+
Bottom Right - $300+
PAGE 201
Top Left - $600+
Top Right - $750+
Middle Left - $225+
Middle Right - $150+
Bottom Left - $8000+
Bottom Right - $300+
PAGE 202
Top Left - $800+
Top Right - $400+
Middle Left - $900+
Middle Right - $7500+
Bottom Left - $200+
Bottom Right - $2500+
PAGE 203
Top Left - $600+
Top Right - $3000+
Middle Left - $400+
Middle Right - $300+
Bottom Left - $4000+
Bottom Right - $150+
PAGE 204
Top Left - $1600+
Top Right - $7000+
Middle Left - $2000+
Middle Right - $6000+
Bottom Left - $8000+
Bottom Right - $4000+

PAGE 205
Top Left - $200+
Top Right - $200+
Middle Left - $200+
Middle Right - Ref. Only
Bottom Left - $300+
Bottom Right - $600+
PAGE 206
Top Left - $3500+
Top Right - $6000+
Middle Left - $7000+
Middle Right - $800+
Bottom Left - $900+
Bottom Right - $300+
PAGE 207
Top Left - $400+
Top Right - $1000+
Middle Left - $1800+
Middle Right - $3000+
Bottom Left - $600+
Bottom Right - $400+
PAGE 208
Top Left -Contemporary
Top Right - Contemporary
Middle Left - $350+
Middle Right - $800+
Bottom Left - $250+
Bottom Right - $900+
PAGE 209
Top Left - $300+
Top Right - $75+
Middle Left - Contemporary
Middle Right - $1200+
Bottom Left - $1600+
Bottom Right-Ref. Only
PAGE 210
Top Left - $700+
Top Right - $1000+
Middle Left - $600+
Middle Right - $3500+
Bottom Left-$200-$500
Bottom Right - $500+
PAGE 211
Top Left - $8000+
Top Right - $5000+
Middle Left - $2500+
Middle Right - $4000+
Bottom Left - $700+
Bottom Right - $2000+
PAGE 212
Top Left - $300+
Top Right - $500+
Middle Left - Contemporary
Middle Right - $800+
Bottom Left - $3000+

Bottom Right -$1800+
& $3000+

PAGE 213
Top Left - $300+
Top Right - $250+
Middle Left - $300+
Middle Right - $300+
Bottom - $250+

PAGE 214
Top Left - $150+
Top Right - $200+
Middle Left - $200+
Middle Right - $300+
Bottom Left - $400+
Bottom Right - $900+

PAGE 215
Top Left - $200+
Top Right - $200+
Middle Left - $400+
Middle Right - $600+
Bottom Left - $600+
Bottom Right - $250+

PAGE 216
Top Left - $800+
Top Right - $800+
Middle Left - $950+
Middle Right - $200+
Bottom Left - $200+
Bottom Right-Ref. Only

PAGE 217
Top Left - $1800+
Top Right - $400+
Middle Left - $650+
Middle Right - $3500+
Bottom Left - $850+
Bottom Right - $200+

PAGE 218
Top Left - $400+
Top Right - $4500+
Middle Left - $1500+
Middle Right - $800+
Bottom Left - $75+
Bottom Right - $200+

PAGE 219
Top Left - $400+
Top Right - Contempo-
rary
Middle Left - Contem-
porary
Middle Right - Contem-
porary
Bottom Left - Contem-
porary
Bottom Right - Contem-
porary

PAGE 220
Top Left - $400+
Top Right - $400+

Middle Left - $1500+
Middle Right - $400+
Bottom Left-$1500+ea
Bottom Right - $3000+

PAGE 221
Top Left - $1800+
Top Right - $5000+
Middle Left - $3000+
Middle Right - $250+
Bottom Left - $100+
Bottom Right - $800+

PAGE 222
Top Left - $2500+
Top Right - $1500+
Middle Left - $5000+
Middle Right - $500+
Bottom Left - $250+
Bottom Right - $800+

PAGE 223
Top Left - $300+
Top Right - $2500+
Middle Left - $3000+
Middle Right - $1000+
Bottom Left - $1250+
Bottom Right - $2500+

PAGE 224
Top Left - $400+
Top Right - $200+ each
Middle Left - $200+
Middle Right - $1200+
Bottom Left - $1800+
Bottom Right - $2000+

PAGE 225
Top Left - $1500+
Top Right - $700+
Middle Left - $1600+
Middle Right - $1200+
Bottom Left - $3000+
Bottom Right - $900+

PAGE 226
Top Left - $2500+
Top Right - $400+
Middle Left - Contem-
porary
Middle Right - Contem-
porary
Bottom Left - $2000+
Bottom Right - $400+

PAGE 227
Top Left - $800+
Top Right - $500+
Middle Left - $400+
Middle Right - $800+
Bottom Left - $100+
Bottom Right - $400+

PAGE 228
Top Left - $200+
Top Right - $500+

Middle Left - $400+
Middle Right - $1000+
Bottom Left - Contem-
porary
Bottom Right - $5000+

PAGE 229
Top - $400+
Middle Left - $10000+
Middle Right -Very Rare
Bottom - Ref. Only

PAGE 230
Top Left - $700+
Top Right - $1500+
Middle Left - $350+
Middle Right - $700+
Bottom Left - $450+
Bottom Right - $500+

PAGE 231
Top Left - $400+
Top Right - $200+
Middle Left - $600+
Middle Right - $3500+
Bottom Left - $3000+
Bottom Right - $900+

PAGE 232
Top Left - $4000+
Top Right - $800+
Middle Left - $2500+
Middle Right - $800+
Bottom Left - $350+
Bottom Right - $250+

PAGE 233
Top Left - $200+
Top Right - $200+
Middle Left - $350+
Middle Right - $300+
Bottom - $450+

PAGE 234
Top Left - $200+
Top Right - $200+
Middle Left - $500+
Middle Right - $500+
Bottom Left - $500+
Bottom Right - $200+

PAGE 235
Top Left - $4000+
Top Right - $800+
Middle Left - $4000+
Middle Right - $1600+
Bottom Left - $2800+
Bottom Right - $200+

PAGE 236
Top - $400+
Middle - $400+
Bottom Left - $350+
Bottom Right - $900+

PAGE 237
Top Left - $300+

Top Right - $400+
2nd Left - $4500+
2nd Right - $1000+
3rd Left - $600+
3rd Right - $300+
Bottom Left - $800+
Bottom Right - $2000+

PAGE 238
Top - $600+
Middle - $11000+
Bottom - $12000+

PAGE 239
Top - $1200+
Middle - $1200+
Bottom - $1500+

PAGE 240
Top - $650+
Middle - $3500+
Bottom - $2000+

PAGE 241
Top - $2500+
Middle - $1200+
Bottom - Priced Earlier

PAGE 242
Top - Ref. Only
Middle - $3000+
Bottom - $8000+

PAGE 243
Top Left - $250+
Top Right - $300+
Middle Left - $250+
Middle Right - $700+
Bottom - Ref. Only

PAGE 244
Top - Ref. Only
Middle - $10000+
Bottom - $900+ $400+

Send pictures no later than July 1, 1992

!!! ATTENTION !!!

We are now working on a book on riding toys other than Pedal Cars. It will include the following:

Tricycles,Wagons,Scooters,Riding Horses,Small Bikes,Sleds,Irish Mail,Etc.

If you would like to have your pictures included in this book Please Send Them In Now.We need SIZE, MAKE, VALUE,Etc.on the back of each picture.If you would like to contribute a group of pictures Please call 1-800-777-6450 and we will send spec. sheets to use, Ask for NEIL,DAVE,or SCOTT.

Send Pictures to:

L-W Books

Box 69

Gas City,IN 46933

WE WILL RETURN PICTURES IF REQUESTED

ALSO WORKING ON NEW BOOK ON

JUKE BOXES

SEND PICTURES IN NOW TO:

L-W BOOKS

BOX 69

GAS CITY,IN 46933

IF YOU WOULD LIKE TO CONTRIBUTE A GROUP OF PIC-TURES CALL 1-800-777-6450 ASK FOR SCOTT OR NEIL

WE WILL RETURN PICTURES IF REQUESTED

IF NEGATIVES ARE AVAILABLE PLEASE SEND THEM ALSO.

ALL CONTRIBUTORS WILL RECEIVE FULL CREDIT IN BOOKS